Bristol's 100 Best Buildings

Publishers' Note
The opinions expressed in this book are those of the author and not necessarily those of the publishers or any of the organisations which have generously supported publication with financial or other support.

The selection of the one hundred buildings is similarly entirely personal to the author.

The sponsorship monies have enabled us to publish in colour throughout and at a more accessible price than would otherwise have been possible.

The organisations to which we are indebted are:

Bristol Civic Society
Bristol Guild
Alec French Architects
AWW
Barton Willmore
Ferguson Mann
JT Group
King Sturge

Collectors' Edition
In addition to the standard softback edition, there is a slip-cased hardback edition, cloth-bound, 100 copies numbered and signed by the author.

Bristol's
100
Best Buildings

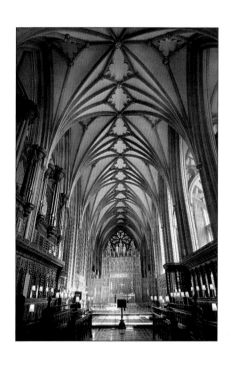

Mike JENNER

Photography: Stephen MORRIS

First published in 2010 by Redcliffe Press Ltd.
81g Pembroke Road, Bristol BS8 3EA

www.redcliffepress.co.uk
info@redcliffepress.co.uk

text © Mike Jenner 2010
photographs and layout © Stephen Morris 2010

Softback edition: ISBN 978-1-906593-61-2

Collectors' edition: ISBN 978-1-906593-67-4

British Library Cataloguing-in-Publication Data
A catalogue record for this book is available from the British Library

Photography, design and typesetting by Stephen Morris www.stephen-morris.com
Printed and bound in the Czech Republic by Akcent Media

FSC
Mixed Sources
Product group from well-managed
forests and other controlled sources

Cert no. SW-COC-003532
www.fsc.org
©1996 Forest Stewardship Council

Opposite: interior, Wills Memorial Tower

Contents

Broad Quay

Introduction

It has been said that to see the development of English architecture in a single town, you should go to Bristol. That is almost certainly true, even though the city has relatively few buildings of national quality and only one of world class, the Cathedral. London has many more of both, but you would have to spend weeks to get around to all you needed to see. In Bristol you could see the lot in a couple of days, and walk to them all. Oxford has more buildings of national quality, but nothing like Bristol's range. Cambridge? York? The list of reasonable candidates is surprisingly short and none compares with Bristol. In a way that is surprising because, as English cities go, Bristol is quite young. The first mention of it – on a coin of all things! – is believed to date from about 1020. But from then it grew rapidly in size and wealth, and wealth always means work for builders. By 1700 it was the second largest city in England. By 1800 however it had started to drop behind, and throughout the nineteenth and twentieth centuries, although it continued to grow, it continued to drop in relative terms. This had the advantage for us of preserving many buildings from the re-development which economic success invariably demands. Large numbers in the centre of the city were lost in the 1940/41 bombing, and in the 1950s and '60s there were grievous losses of minor Georgian buildings and major Victorian ones. In those years the conservation movement was barely beginning and the great majority of people were uninterested in architecture and heartily despised everything made in Victoria's reign. However, by luck more than policy, Bristol has retained buildings from every period since the Conquest.

Bristol has a population of around half a million if we include areas like Filton, Patchway and Kingswood that are outside Bristol proper. On the crudest of crude estimations, that means something of the order of 100,000 buildings. I can't pretend to have seen all those, or even to have been down all the streets, but the Department of National Heritage has listed 2,129 of what they consider the best, and I know most of them and all the important ones. (The list includes many minor structures such as boundary walls, telephone kiosks etc.) Out of the whole lot I have chosen 100, not all of them on the Department's list. They are a personal choice and

anybody making a similar one would choose differently. My list immediately raises questions – is 38 College Green, for example, which is included, 'better' than Brislington parish church, which is not? The answer, of course, is that it isn't, but I have tried to include the best representative examples of the various building types and architectural styles. 38 College Green is in because it has the most beautiful Art Nouveau façade in Bristol. The delightful Brislington church is out because the church at Westbury-on-Trym is of about the same date and style and equally attractive, but historically more important (and it has Bristol's most delightful churchyard). I haven't, however, included any building merely because it's representative of something: every one of those chosen is fascinating and all are a great pleasure to look at, but I have occasionally allowed prominence to affect my choice. The Council House on College Green is the building about which I dithered most. I finally decided to include it because of its prominence and its few good qualities, but also to point out some of its absurdities. I have tried to avoid using technical terms as much as possible, but when I do I explain them in the short glossary which follows this introduction. In most cases the context should make them clear, and reference to the adjoining photograph will help.

I have been cavalier in deciding what a 'building' is. Most of the entries describe a single building, but I also include several terraces, streets and squares when the group has an individuality of its own, separate from the buildings which make it up. I also devote one of the entries to Bristol's famous eighteenth-century wrought-ironwork. Two bridges have made it into the list.

I have graded each building by giving it from one to five stars. This is even more subjective than choosing the hundred, and shouldn't be taken too seriously, but it does identify the buildings which in my opinion no lover of architecture should miss. Some with five stars are so obvious they need no recommendation, but some, like the Bank of England branch in Corn Street, are very little known and yet of superlative quality. I haven't given stars to the buildings erected in the post-war period because I can't be sufficiently objective, most of them having been designed by friends or people I knew. Entries are arranged chronologically, so that the book can be read as a history of architecture in Bristol and therefore to some extent as a history of English architecture.

Some readers will want to know more about Bristol's architecture than this book can supply. There is a list of relevant Redcliffe Press titles in print at the back. Timothy Mowl's studies are brilliantly written, always entertaining as well as being scholarly, Andrew Foyle's wonderful volume in the Pevsner series cannot be too highly recommended and it's very cheap, but the ultimate is the big (and unfortunately not cheap) *Bristol: an architectural history*, which Andor Gomme, Bryan Little and I co-wrote thirty years ago. A new edition, substantially re-written by Andor and me, is imminent. The book you are reading now is a taster.

The following fourteen buildings are graded with 5 stars:

  Bank of England, Broad Street
  Blaise Hamlet, Henbury
  Brunel's Temple Meads Station
  Bush Warehouse, Prince Street
  Cathedral, College Green
  Clifton Suspension Bridge
  Concrete House, Westbury-on-Trym
  Exchange, Corn Street
  Granary, Welsh Back
  King's Weston House
  Library, College Green
  St Mary Redcliffe
  Wesley's New Room, Broadmead and
  Wills Memorial Tower.

The thirty-one buildings graded with 4 stars are of only slightly less importance.

Mike Jenner. Bristol, October 2010

Acknowledgements

My debt to previous writers on Bristol's architecture, including those mentioned in my introduction, is obviously enormous. Several of the architects of the 15 post-war buildings included in the book gave me vital information, and two or three read and commented on what I had written about their building. My daughter Caroline and my son Adam read my first draft, which at that time didn't contain Stephen's splendid photographs to make the task enjoyable. I am deeply grateful to them all.

Mike Jenner

A note about the photography

So many people let me photograph the buildings in their keep and one or two joined me to stand on high balconies; I can't thank them enough. Almost all the photographs were captured digitally, some on transparency film. Afterwards, I polished them as one would a print in the darkroom: dodging, burning and cropping to produce the final image.

Stephen Morris

Glossary

Arcade: a row of arches supported by columns or piers.

Arts and Crafts: movement inspired by William Morris to revive handicrafts generally, and in architecture to use traditional crafts and materials. Flourished in England throughout the second half of the nineteenth century. Influential in Europe and America after around 1900.

Ashlar: walling where the faces of the stones are dressed smooth.

Baroque: European art of the seventeenth century and a little later. In English and French architecture it was governed by a considerable amount of classical restraint.

Capital: the terminating feature at the top of a column, pilaster or pier.

Chancel: eastern part of the church reserved for the clergy, originally the financial responsibility of the diocese, not the parish.

Chantry: It was believed that a soul's removal from purgatory into heaven could be accelerated by the prayers of the faithful on earth. Chantries were endowments to support one or more priests to pray in perpetuity for the release of the souls of specified individuals. Such endowments often included the money to pay for the erection of chapels for this purpose. The larger churches had many chantry chapels. All English chantries were suppressed in 1547.

Classical: a word which has gathered too many meanings. Strictly it applies to the arts of ancient Greece and Rome, more loosely to buildings using Greek or Roman forms, e.g. columns, entablatures, pediments etc. From this the meaning has been extended to works of art governed by the spirit of classical art, but not using its forms. An excellent example is Bank House (q.v.). (The popular use of the word is often ridiculous; much 'classical' music, for instance, is not in the least classical)

Clerestory: the part of a church's nave walls containing windows above the roofs of the aisles.

Console: an ornamental S-curved classical bracket.

Cornice: top projecting element of a classical entablature.

Cove: a concave moulding, usually forming part of a cornice, sometimes very large.

Crossing: in a church with transepts, the space between them, the nave and the chancel.

Decorated Gothic: the period of English architecture from the mid-thirteenth century to the mid-fourteenth century.

Domestic Revival: beginning in the 1870s and '80s as an aspect of the Arts and Crafts Movement, it had a late flowering in Bristol, producing a crop of buildings in the years around 1900.

Early English: Gothic architecture c.1190-1250.

Elevation: the face of a building, more strictly a scale drawing of it.

Entablature: the series of mouldings supported by classical columns or doorways, windows etc.

Gadroon: a heavily scalloped curved surface.

Gothic: in England the architectural style of c.1190-1530, characterised by pointed arches.

Gothick: spelling used by the early Gothic revivalists and used to denote buildings of that period.

Hammerbeam: short timbers projecting from the top of the wall to support vertical hammer posts and roof braces. Brunel used an imitation hammerbeam roof in his Temple Meads train shed (q.v.).

Laudian: church furnishings introduced during Archbishop Laud's 1630s anti-Puritan campaign.

Lesene: a pilaster without base, cap or tapering. Can take the form of a vertical strip of quoins.

Lunette: a semi-circular window or other opening.

Machicolation: a gallery or parapet bracketed out from the top of a defensive wall, with openings in its floor to drop boiling oil etc. on enemies.

Modillion cornice: one supported on little cubic brackets.

Mullion: a vertical stone or wooden support dividing a window into separate lights.

Narthex: an ante-chamber at the entrance of a church.

Nave: the main body of a church, the financial responsibility of the parish.

Orders: classical architecture was based on five orders – Doric, Ionic, Corinthian, Tuscan and Composite, the first three being much the most popular. Each had its own columns, entablature and proportions. Where they are mentioned here the photograph will identify them.

Oriel: a projecting, overhanging window.

Orientation: Where possible churches were built on an east/west axis, with the high altar at the east end. Descriptions always talk of the west front, east end etc., and ignore the actual orientation, which can sometimes be very different.

Palladianism: English eighteenth-century architects, more than those of any other country, were influenced by the buildings and books of Andrea Palladio, and under the influence of such figures as Lord Burlington tended to reduce architecture to a matter of rules. Buildings and their details were either 'correct' or 'incorrect'.

Pavilion (in classical buildings): parts of a façade projecting forward, usually at centre and ends.

Pediment: the triangular feature crowning a classical portico, window or door etc.

Perpendicular Gothic: English architecture of the period from the mid-fourteenth century to the early sixteenth century.

Picturesque: originally a landscape reminiscent of a painting by Claude, Salvator Rosa etc., then by extension, an important aesthetic movement extolling the wild, rugged and 'terrible'. It originated in England but soon conquered Europe and America.

Pier: a heavy masonry support, as distinct from a slimmer column.

Pilaster: a flat column, projecting slightly from a wall.

Putti: naked or lightly draped children, usually 'supporting' human figures, coats of arms, etc.

Quoins: large squared stones used to strengthen, actually or visually, the corners of buildings.

Reredos: screen, usually sculpted but sometimes painted, rising up behind the altar.

Rococo: the last phase of the baroque. In Britain most frequently used in interior decoration and furnishing, but rarely used externally.

Romanesque architecture: the western European style from c.700 till the advent of Gothic. It is typified by round arches. [Often called Norman architecture]

Romanticism, romantic: Europe-wide art and literary movement of the decades on either side of 1800. The Picturesque was one of its aspects.

Rubble stonework: walls constructed of stones left uncut as delivered from the quarry.

Rustication: masonry cut in large blocks with recessed joints. There were numerous types.

Transepts: the arms projecting on either side of a church, thus giving it a cruciform shape.

Transom: a horizontal stone or wooden member dividing, with the mullions, a window into separate lights.

Voussoir: the splayed stones or bricks making a flat or curved arch. Their strength derives from the weight above being converted by their shape into a horizontal force which has to be resisted by the walling on each side, or by some other force such as that from another arch.

Redland Chapel

The Ionic pilasters support an entablature of which the cornice (the projecting top member) rests on little brackets called modillions. The cornice is the bottom member of the triangular pediment. The turret has its own cornice, supported on console brackets. The ridged shaping of the lead dome is called gadrooning (more usually seen in silverware than architecture).

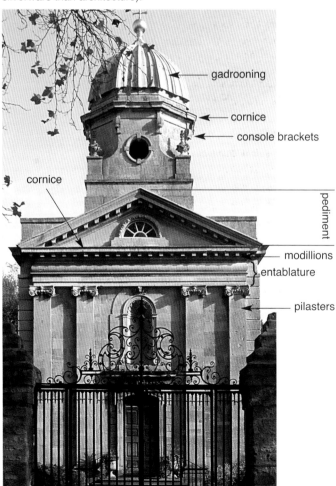

The Chapter House, Bristol Cathedral

Bristol's 100 Best Buildings
in chronological order

Bristol Cathedral ★★★★★
Main building periods c1140, 1230, 1298-1330, 1867-77, 1887-8

The cathedral is the only building in the city which is indisputably of world class; its chancel is known, if only from photographs, by students of architectural history from Tokyo to New York. Like most English cathedrals it grew piecemeal over many centuries and parts of it survive from all the main architectural periods.

The Chapter House
Again like many English cathedrals, Bristol's began as a monastery (in fact as an abbey of Augustinian canons, who were priests, not monks, but living a monastic life). Their Abbey was founded in about 1140. Only a few bits of that building survive, the best of which is the room where the canons held their business meetings – the Chapter House. It dates from a decade or two after the founding of the Abbey, and is in the Anglo-Norman branch of what we now call the Romanesque style of architecture.

The Chapter House is wonderfully eloquent, transporting us from today into a different and frightening world. It is a simple rectangular vaulted hall of no very compelling character as far as its shape or proportions are concerned, but it over-awes the visitor with the shallow carved decoration which covers the walls like a Polynesian's tattoos. Originally it was coloured and would have had much more savage power. The ornaments are routine late-Norman details – interlaced arcades, chevrons and so on but repeated obsessively over every available vertical surface. The Chapter House looks back to an ancient and more terrifying world which still occupies a dim corner of our minds, but which in the twelfth century was a part of everyday life.

It was built to house the deliberations of churchmen, but it echoes with the terrors of the dark forest and the cold northern seas. The genteel modern interventions come close to spoiling its character, such as the comfy parquet flooring which is ludicrously domestic in this barbaric interior, and the great glaring sheets of etched plate glass in the windows, which almost destroy its mystery. Yet it would be hard to find an interior which conveys so vividly one side of the Norman character – uncouth vigour and toughness.

But the Anglo-Norman architects could achieve a wider emotional range than the carving suggests. The Chapter House is entered from a small vestibule which is three arches wide and two deep, so that there are four free-standing columns to support the vaulting. The space is constricted by the closeness of the columns, and low because there is another room above it within the same height as the Chapter House. The sense of release after passing through this tight and shadowed complexity into the much larger open space of the Chapter House is intense, and was clearly designed to have this effect upon people. Together as a sequence the two rooms achieve an extraordinarily high level of expressiveness. Many later buildings of an infinitely greater polish and sophistication are by comparison inexpressive, indeed dumb.

The roof of the Chapter House is an early example of a rib vault (a vault with projecting stone ribs at the junctions of the curved surfaces), and some of the arches in the vestibule are pointed, two of the main distinguishing characteristics of the next architectural style – the Gothic. But details don't make a style and there is nothing remotely Gothic in these rooms; they are late-Norman Romanesque built at a time when the new style had begun in France and was about to appear in England.

The Elder Lady Chapel
The first appearance in Bristol of the new Gothic style was in 1230 when the canons built onto the College Green side of their abbey the older of the two Lady Chapels. The change from Norman Romanesque to what we now call Gothic began in France in about 1140 and was established in England when the choir at Canterbury Cathedral was begun in 1177. Hardly surprisingly since it was designed by a Frenchman, Canterbury is still very French in appearance. But nobody could mistake the next steps, Lincoln, Salisbury or Wells cathedrals, all

begun in the years around 1220, for anything but English buildings. The Bristol Elder Lady Chapel is a tiny but wonderful work in this Early English Gothic. Only three generations separate it from the Chapter House, but the change in spirit is an unbridgeable gulf. In the Chapter House the savage decoration covers the walls but it doesn't transform them: they remain just walls, flat and inert. In the Lady Chapel the decoration transforms the walls into a complex three-dimensional structure which pulsates with energy and life. The Chapel is eloquent of a happier and newer world. It is profoundly spiritual and yet deeply human, even earthy in some of its carvings. It is the perfect embodiment in stone of that golden moment in the early thirteenth century when St Francis was addressing all animate creation as brother and sister.

The chancel and nave

As time passed and the canons' wealth increased from the legacies of the pious, they were bound to want a larger, more up-to-date church. So in 1298 they started a major rebuilding, beginning with the chancel so that the temporarily walled-off nave remained usable. When work was complete in 1330, the Abbey consisted of the Norman nave and chapter house, and the Gothic chancel and Lady Chapel. Then the money ran out and work didn't start again until 1470, when they demolished the nave, built the transepts and the rather uninspiring tower over the crossing. They had barely started the walls of the new nave when work stopped again and didn't re-start for 400 years. The tiny stump of a building remained without a nave until 1868 when George Street's present one was started. By then English monasticism was long in the past and the abbey had become a cathedral. Street's work is often criticised, I think unfairly. He continued the chancel's pattern, but with slight variations to ensure that nobody would think the two were contemporary. After his death the uninteresting west front with its two towers was built in 1887-8 to the design of J. L. Pearson, a terrible disappointment to anyone who knows his Truro Cathedral.

It is understandable that through all those years it was St Mary Redcliffe, the largest parish church in Britain, of which Bristolians were proud and which historians praised. Until the middle of the twentieth century nobody ever doubted that it was Bristol's really great medieval building. Then opinion reversed; today it is the

cathedral, and particularly its chancel, which attracts most attention. There were two main reasons for this shift, which are complex but worth examination because they go to the heart of our appreciation of architecture. The first is that we – far more than any earlier generations – value originality. The second arose from the fact that the modern movement has accustomed us to admire particularly the complex modelling of space. Originality and spatial complexity are the two outstanding qualities of the cathedral's chancel. We know nothing of the master mason who designed it, not even his name, but we can feel close to him because his design personality was so powerful, and seems to us so modern. Like all geniuses he was a child of his time: one has no difficulty, for example, in dating his work, which is another way of saying that in some ways it is typical of its date. It is Decorated Gothic, or Middle Pointed as the Victorians called it. But while most of the details are typical of their time, they are put together in original ways. Sometimes the result can only be described as wilful, perverse and sometimes even ugly, but they add up to a totality which

left:
North wall of the Elder
Lady Chapel

right:
Vaulting in the chancel's
south aisle

Looking up at the ceiling of the Berkeley Chapel's ante-room, where the flat stone slabs are supported by flying ribs

The nave, looking towards the crossing

to our eyes is intensely exciting and stimulating.

In some buildings the space within the walls and ceiling, rather than the design of their surfaces, is what provides the kicks. This only happens when the space is moulded in some way; when there are hints that it continues round corners, or when it is partially screened so that there are vistas through from one space to another. This experience is appreciated most by walking through the spaces, enjoying the constantly shifting vistas, and the journeys which the eye takes in exploring the spaces which come into view, develop, and then disappear as one moves.

In most churches relatively low aisles were built on one or both sides of the high nave, thus dividing the interior into separate but visually connected spaces. At the Abbey the master mason persuaded the Abbott to build his aisles as high as the chancel, making the interior into a single huge space. This type of design, now called a hall church, later became common in Germany, though it never caught on in England. By 1300 in the greater churches, for example at St Mary Redcliffe, it was routine for the high vault to be supported by buttresses flying over the roofs of the aisles. That obviously couldn't be done here, but support was necessary because the outward thrust of the vaults over the wide chancel was greater than the counter-balancing thrust of the narrower aisle vaults. So the master built stone bridges between the columns and the side walls, which had the same effect. Ordinary but heavy buttresses outside the building were sufficient to counter-balance the outward thrust of the aisle vaults and the bridges.

So far I have been describing the mechanics of the structure, but the reason for using it was the aesthetic advantage it brought to the interior. As one wanders through the cathedral it becomes apparent that the Bristol master particularly liked stone ribs flying unsupported through space. There is a famous example in the tiny ante-room of the Berkeley Chapel, where the flat stone slabs of the ceiling are supported by flying ribs. There is no structural justification for this minute tour-de-force, it is purely a love of the exciting spatial experience. The master used his aisle bridges to do something similar, bringing his stone vault down to a point midway across each bridge, and then omitting the usual stone webs between the ribs. The effect of all this (which is impossible to describe adequately in words) is an extraordinary spatial complexity. One's eye is invited to go on many different voyages of exploration, looking up

The Eastern Lady Chapel

between the numerous high columns, going through the bridges and the voids in the vaulting above them. As one walks through the building (and the Victorian nave uses the same structure) the views are constantly changing. This is an architecture which can never be adequately captured by drawings or still photographs, only by the movie camera. Its full appreciation had to wait 600 years for the age of the movie and the sensibility which accompanies it.

Not all the fireworks scintillate overhead: the Eastern Lady Chapel (behind the main altar) is an astounding display of the master's virtuosity, now a glorious explosion of colour owing to its repainting in the early twentieth century under the direction of Professor Tristram. He worked from a few faded traces of original paint, to which he added an artist's eye for colour and a willingness to invent when evidence was lacking: nowadays an abomination to pedants but a glory to anybody with a fully operating pair of eyes. If only the Chapter House could be similarly decorated – but it won't happen in our time: the pedants now rule.

The exterior of the building is relatively dull: the master had sacrificed a dramatic display of flying but-

tresses to gain one of the most exciting interiors of his time. There are too many examples of his originality and wilfulness to be described here – his extraordinary use of what look like upside-down arches on top of normal ones; his use of straight lines in curvilinear window tracery, and so on. Usually he gets away with it, but sometimes it is quite extraordinarily jarring. It is the price which has to be paid for the originality which brought his great successes. He was one of that type of artist who dislikes ready-made solutions, and who cannot accept all the values of his own time. Such rebels have it much too easy nowadays, and in consequence are ten-a-penny, but before the Romantic period it was very hard for them and they were consequently rare. In the medieval period the Bristol master was almost unique. We can now appreciate that his cathedral is not merely the finest building in Bristol, but one of the great buildings of the world.

St Mary Redcliffe ★★★★★

Mainly thirteenth, fourteenth and fifteenth centuries
Spire 1870-72

'The fairest, goodliest and most famous parish church in our Realm.' Queen Elizabeth's soundbite may be apocryphal but it is accurate. There are one or two parish churches elsewhere which, depending on how you measure, are of similar or slightly greater square

Externally the nave, chancel and transepts, supported by their flying buttresses, rise high above the aisles. The ensemble is superb, and superb in a typically English way – a collection of separate elements which heap up together to make a wonderful whole. It is more like the unity of a marvellously coherent village than the unity, say, of a French cathedral. Considering that the dates range from the late thirteenth century to the early fifteenth century the impression of uniformity is

footage, but none of them comes even close to St Mary Redcliffe's soaring cathedral-like magnificence. It owes its splendour to the piety and wealth of the merchants who paid for it, but it needed to be big, as St Mary Mancroft in Norwich and its other competitors for size did not. By about 1150 half Bristol's population lived in Redcliffe in Somerset, separate from Bristol which was in Gloucestershire. St Mary Redcliffe was founded at some unknown date before 1158, and had to serve a population equal to that of the dozen or so parishes then in Bristol. Although the pressure of numbers was somewhat eased when the parish of St Thomas's was created, during the next 300 years St Mary Redcliffe was rebuilt, bit by bit, on an even grander scale.

remarkable. In fact the date range is greater than that because the spire was hit by lightning in 1446 and all but a short stump destroyed. The church remained in this mutilated condition for nearly 450 years, until 1872 when it was rebuilt to a design believed to be an accurate replacement of the original, though of course there was no way of knowing exactly what that was apart from the evidence of the stump. Reaching 292 feet into the sky, the thirteenth-century tower and its 'fourteenth-century' spire are the greatest glory of south Bristol's townscape.

Of the smaller elements which make up the exterior of St Mary Redcliffe, the most brilliant and intriguing is the fourteenth-century north porch, which faced down the hill to Redcliffe Gate a hundred yards or so away. It is intriguing because there was already a perfectly good porch in that location, dating from the previous century. During their constant rebuilding, the parish would probably have demolished it as they had demolished so much else, but its west wall is part of the substructure of the tower, and it would be a bold man, even today, who would tamper with that. So they built a new porch onto the front of the old one. It is therefore a bit lower down the hill and requires steps at the junction. There

1330. Since it displays the same sort of originality and boldness of conception it seems reasonable to assume that the Abbey's master mason or some of his team moved on from one to the other. The porch is hexagonal, with its south side built onto the north side of the old one, and it is two storeys high. The entrance is a single volume, but so high that there is room for a row of windows above the doorway. Externally this means that the lower storey looks like two. In complete contrast,

The northern transept and porch

couldn't have been much practical reason for the additional porch because it simply elongates the old one, making the two into a sort of corridor with a flight of steps halfway along its length. It has been suggested that the outer porch served as a pilgrimage shrine, and perhaps it did, but it would be hard to think of a more inconvenient place to put it: a few people praying or chatting can cause as much obstruction in a long corridor as in a short one. Much the most probable reason was the desire to create a landmark to welcome parishioners coming up from Redcliffe.

Like so much of the church, the exact date of the new porch is unknown, but it is probably roughly contemporary with the ending of work at the cathedral in about

the upper storey (containing the room made famous by the boy-poet Chatterton) is kept very low, with continuous strip windows interrupted only by the buttresses at the angles. The windows are set back behind the wall surface of the lower storey by an enormous sloping window cill. Above the windows is a low pierced balustrade, again set well back by another great slope of stone. This series of sloping set-backs produces a pyramidal building of enormous complexity and originality. The great Victorian architect E. W. Godwin thought the pyramidal shape called out for a pyramidal roof, and believed that the unknown designer had intended one. Sir George Oatley, who restored the porch in the 1930s, and a subsequent distinguished architect to the fabric,

Alan Rome, both thought the same. It is regrettable that no Victorian patron decided to commission one. It won't happen now, with our unquestioning belief that old buildings should never be altered.

When you look at the extraordinary carving on the outer porch it is easy to see why the Victorians called the architecture of that period Decorated, and when you go into the church to see why they called the architecture of the later fifteenth century Perpendicular. The entire church is stone-vaulted, and the aisles run right round the nave, around the transepts and round the choir, a veritable forest of stone, opening a multitude of diagonal views in every direction. The soaring height is emphasised by the narrowness of the nave and choir, probably dictated by the dimensions of the earlier church which was being rebuilt bit by bit. You can see the progress of the rebuilding if you compare the south aisle and transept, which are Decorated, with the rest, which is Perpendicular. In the Decorated work it is fascinating to observe quirky and unsettling details like those in the cathedral, such as the use of straight lines in arched windows, and to realise that they, like the porch, date from around the time work there finished.

Discussion of the church cannot omit mention of some outstanding internal features. The tombs and monuments need a rewarding day to themselves; the superlative eighteenth-century ironwork is described later in a separate entry. The roof bosses are easily missed: there are more than 1100 of them, many Christian in subject matter, some secular, a few profane, but every one different and carved with a prodigality of invention which is hard for modern people to understand. Those in the aisles are low enough to be appreciated quite easily, but medieval congregations, without the benefit of binoculars, could hardly see those in the high vaults. They were carved for the glory of God and the satisfaction of the carvers, not the examination of the parishioners.

The last century has not been kind to St Mary Redcliffe. Until well into the nineteenth century it arose dramatically from a tangle of narrow streets, riding high above the little houses. Today it is diminished by the great open spaces of road and car park on its northern side, and the traffic thundering past its western front.

The southern side

Holy Trinity ★★ Westbury-on-Trym
Early thirteenth century, late fifteenth century

Westbury-on-Trym is one of the villages which became embedded into the ever-expanding city. Its parish church is set on the steep hill which rises up from the little river Trym and the tangle of ancient streets below. The churchyard climbing up from the church is an enchantment: the perfect picturesque mix of kempt and unkempt, wild vegetation and roughly mown grass, gently decaying stonework and tottering tombstones. Its upkeep is a model to incumbents and churchwardens everywhere.

Westbury-on-Trym is older than Bristol, appearing in documents centuries before there is any record of Bricgstow. Possibly by 720 and certainly by 803 there was a Benedictine monastery at Westbury, its church almost certainly the precursor of this one. About 50 generations of villagers have been buried here; untold thousands of people. Archaeologists say that centuries of burials are the reason why the levels of ancient churchyards are al-

ways higher than the surrounding gardens or streets, often by as much as ten feet. The phenomenon is cloaked here by the rising hillside, but it must have contributed to the rise in the ground on the southern side of the church.

In the thirteenth century, when neighbouring Bristol had far outgrown little Westbury, the ambitious Bishop Giffard of Worcester, in whose diocese Bristol then was, enlarged the church and tried to establish it as his second cathedral on the precedent of Bath and Wells. It came to nothing. Then, in the mid-fifteenth century, Bishop Carpenter made another attempt, equally unsuccessful.

The interior of this relatively modest church which so nearly became a cathedral is a satisfyingly large airy space dominated by windows filled with Victorian stained glass, some of it very enjoyable. Those at the east end are almost too garish in colour but make the interior

remarkably cheerful. In many churches stained glass has the grave disadvantage of darkening the interior. Here that is not a problem because in the late fifteenth century the nave was heightened to provide windows above the aisle arcades, and they have clear glass which floods the interior with light. The arcades themselves date from the early thirteenth century.

Externally the church is pleasant rather than stunning, with a good deal of alteration and restoration which has left mysterious blocked doors and unexplained bits of ornament in the walls. The Perpendicular tower has the typical Bristol feature of a stair turret which is higher and more elaborate than the other pinnacles. Here it finishes with an octagon and a high concave pinnacle, all in open-work (rebuilt, apparently faithfully, in the nineteenth century). Seated in a niche in his tower Bishop Carpenter glowers down at the car park, and in the chancel his grim cadaver, which he intended should be a reminder to future generations of the transience of the worldly power he enjoyed in life (he combined his diocesan duties with being Chancellor of Oxford University as well as Provost of Oriel) has been discreetly cloaked by a heavy Victorian stone casing through which the representation of his decayed and shrivelled corpse can only be glimpsed. Probably very few people ever crouch down to see it now.

The Lord Mayor's Chapel ★★★ College Green
Thirteenth century, fourteenth century
Sometimes known as St Mark's or The Gaunts

The Chapel, dedicated to St Mark, was built by Maurice de Gaunt in about 1230 as part of an almshouse called the Hospital of St Mark. Because it was run by the Abbey it was suppressed in 1539 with all the other monasteries. The canons got pensions, the resident almsmen were given a few pence and thrown onto the street. Two years later, in 1539, the Corporation bought, at a knock-down price in this buyers' market of huge amounts of monastic land, the estates and buildings, including the Chapel which then appears to have been used as a sort of supernumerary parish church. When the Huguenot refugees arrived in Bristol it was granted to them. In 1721 the Corporation fell out with the Dean and Chapter and decided to stop worshipping in the cathedral and use St Mark's instead. Thereafter it was known as the Mayor's Chapel, until 1898 when the Bristol mayors were promoted and it became the Lord Mayor's Chapel. Much restoration was carried out in 1889 by the architect J. L. Pearson.

When the church was built, the site boundaries at the time presumably didn't allow the normal east-west orientation, so, somewhat unusually, it is oriented roughly north-south, with the altar at the north. (To avoid confusion, the following notes will use conventional orientation, so actual south will be called west, and so on.) The nave dates from around 1230, the chancel from about 1500, the south aisle about 1280, a chapel opening off it about 1510, the Poyntz Chapel at the far east end 1523, and the tower, with its typically high Bristol spire-like pinnacle set at one corner over the stair, was completed in 1487, as recorded, very unusually, in a mason's inscription. In the fifteenth century the west window was replaced by a Perpendicular one, and this in turn was replaced in 1822 when a peculiarly horrible new front was built facing onto College Green. In 1889 the front was again rebuilt, with a reasonable version of the original Perpendicular window.

The topography of the site is now almost entirely obscured by buildings, and the easing of the gradient of Park Street when it was bridged over the much more ancient Frogmore Lane, but the Chapel is built into the steeply sloping north side of a small hill which includes the cathedral and the Public Library. In order to get a

level floor from end to end the builders had to set the floor several metres below the level of College Green. This means that on entering one has to go down steps to reach floor level. The view looking down the long, high, narrow church that greets one is extremely pleasant, dominated by the lovely dark brown and gold oak roof.

The side aisle is most interesting for its monuments, but the Poyntz Chapel of Jesus, hidden away through a door at the back, is a small, but delightful treasure, possibly the last bit of medieval church building in Bristol, but a distressing monument to the vanity of human wishes. It was built during his lifetime by Sir Robert Poyntz, who had been with the king at the Field of Cloth of Gold. In his will of 1520 he said the chapel was not quite finished and instructed his executors to complete it and 'garnish the said chapel and certain images and the altar of the same with altar cloths, vestments, book and chalice and all other things thereunto necessary.' The master of the Hospital was to have the income from several manors:

> to provide an honest and considerable priest to sing mass at the altar [in perpetuity] ... the said priest to have for his salary £6 [per annum]. A solemn obit is to be kept for my soul in the said church of the Gaunts [each year] on the day of my departing; in the evening placebo and dirige by note [sung vespers for the dead and a dirge] .... and 6s 8d sterling to be distributed in alms to the poor. The said priest shall always be tabled and lodged within the house of the Gaunts.

Alas, only 20 years after the chapel was completed all the English chantries were suppressed. Poyntz's images were destroyed, his altar cloths, vestments, book, chalice and manors confiscated, all on the orders, and for the profit, of the king whose arms he had so proudly carved, with his own, on the vault above his tomb. Even the tomb itself is lost because it was destroyed when his burial vault below it collapsed in 1730.

St John's-on-the-Wall ★★★★ Broad Street

Late fourteenth century, late fifteenth century
Now redundant, vested in the Churches Conservation Trust

The smallest and one of the most fascinating of Bristol's medieval churches, St John's is the only survivor of the five built over gates in the Norman town wall, much of which became redundant when the Frome was diverted in the 1240s, and new walls were built to enclose a much larger area. (The other wall churches were St Nicholas's of which the crypt still survives, and the three long-lost churches of St Giles's, St Leonard's and St Lawrence's, the last of which was next door to St John's and shared

its steeple and gate.) Although nothing of the wall is now visible above ground, its line is still very clear, and wonderfully evocative, marked by the narrow streets which run along its inside face – Bell Lane, St Leonard's Lane and Tower Lane. St John's tower and spire surmount the gateway which was the entry for people coming across Frome Bridge into Bristol from the north. Naive figures of Brennus and Belinus, Bristol's mythical founders, sit in niches on either side of its central arch.

The church is very narrow because its site, being bounded by Tower Lane on one side and Gropecunte Lane on the other (renamed Nelson Street by a more solemn age), was restricted to not much more than the width of the wall. It consists of a lower crypt-like church which is at road level and dedicated to the Holy Cross, and the main church above, dedicated to St John the Baptist. In the lower church the western two bays were paid for by Walter Frampton who died in 1388, and the three smaller eastern bays were built slightly earlier. This part of the church contained the guild and chantry chapels for which there was no room above. The upper church's nave was also built by Walter Frampton, and its chancel rebuilt in the late fifteenth century. Nave and chancel are in effect a single long room lit on each side by four Perpendicular windows in the nave and two in the chancel, over one of which is a smaller window which lit the long-removed rood screen which originally divided the space. The separate function of the chancel was emphasized by a slightly more elaborate timber roof than the one over the nave. The effigy of Walter Frampton still lies on his monument with his dog at his feet and angels at his head, though now moved from a central position into a side recess.

St John's contains the best collection of Laudian church fittings in Bristol: a wonderfully complicated cross-shaped font of 1624, a communion table dated 1635, rails of about 1650, a brass lectern of perhaps 1670 and a gallery of about the same date with charmingly naive painted panels; beside the pulpit there was until recently an iron hour-glass large enough to alert a restive congregation, now in storage.

Early Bristol took its water from the two rivers and a few springs. The town (not yet a city) was given clean

The font of 1624

St Stephen's ★★★★   St Stephen's Avenue
Thirteenth century, c1480

Many writers on Bristol's history have enthused about the splendour of the city's parish churches, which before the war was very real, though it certainly isn't now to anywhere near the same degree. But St Mary Redcliffe, St Stephen's and the rest blinded them to the curious fact that the number of Bristol's churches never approached that of other towns of similar size and wealth, but much greater antiquity. In 1150 or just after, there were 12 in Bristol, whilst Norwich and Winchester each had 57, and even little Worcester 22. After the foundation of St Stephen's in about 1240, no new parish church was built in Bristol until St Paul's was begun in 1794, a period of 550 years.

St Stephen's was originally built in the thirteenth century as an offshoot of Glastonbury Abbey, probably to serve the new area created in the 1240s when the Frome was diverted into its present channel. It was almost completely rebuilt in about 1480 and nothing of the first church survives except the lower part of the north aisle wall, presumably to save its fourteenth-century tombs. Like many churches of the late fifteenth century its lofty nave and chancel are a single space. The details are of that rather routine and repetitive Perpendicular which was so popular in the later fifteenth century. As a result the interior, though impressive, is slightly disappointing. That might also be due in part to the fact that much of it was rebuilt after a devastating storm in 1703 brought three pinnacles from the top of the tower crashing through the roof, presumably smashing the windows, most of which look as though they date from the eighteenth or nineteenth centuries.

St Stephen's is notable for its tower and its bells, not for its interior. It has been called one of the famous Somerset group of towers, but although it does have a few typically Somerset details, it is in fact quite foreign. The most obvious departure from the Somerset style is the cresting on the roof, which derives from Gloucester cathedral. There are three parish churches in Somerset which have this magnificent crown, so on its own that would not disqualify it as one of the Somerset group. What makes it so foreign is its skinny proportion, almost unique in English medieval architecture, and the antithesis of the sturdy, enormously strong-looking, Somerset

piped water in the thirteenth century, nearly all of it engineered by the several religious houses. The Carmelite Friary, on the present site of the Colston Hall, piped its water from a spring now just below the top of Park Street (still identified by tiny inscribed concrete markers set into the pavement on the west side of the street). In the fourteenth century the water was made more conveniently available to Bristolians by an extension of the pipe across Frome Bridge to a public conduit at St John's (moved a few feet in 1827 to its present position on the church's wall facing Nelson Street). For a few terrible days during the 1940/41 blitz all central Bristol's water mains except the Carmelites' supply to St John's Conduit were cut. Another generation of Bristolians had to rely on water from pipes laid by the friars 700 years earlier.

This mid-nineteenth-century photograph emphasises the slimness of the tower. [*In Search of the Picturesque: the Early English Photographs of JWG Gutch*, Ian Sumner, Redcliffe/Westcliffe Books 2010]

towers. In some ways it is like a tall Italian campanile clad in English Perpendicular ornament (which sounds horrible, but in fact isn't).

Until the twentieth century most views of the tower were of its upper stages appearing over the roofs of the surrounding houses and the masts of the ships in the adjacent harbour. When seen in that way it is brilliantly effective. It seems likely (to an architect who has faced similar requests) that Benet Crosse, the mason, was asked to design a prodigy tower of maximum height and richness on a relatively limited budget. Something had to go, so he sacrificed width for height and splurged on the elaboration of the most visible part, the upper stage and the cresting. St Stephen's has the highest medieval tower in Bristol (obviously excluding the spire of St Mary Redcliffe) and is only exceeded in Somerset by the central tower of Wells cathedral. It is a landmark which has been loved through all the changes of fashion from the moment it was complete, and was a gift from the Bristol merchant and mayor John Shipward.

Very little or none of the external stonework of the church is likely to be original because it has been refaced several times after stone decay became offensive. The glorious eighteenth-century ironwork inside the church, from the blitzed St Nicholas's, is described later in a separate entry.

Red Lodge ★★★   Park Row
1577-85

Now the Red Lodge Museum

The sixteenth century is the only one since the twelfth to have left little more than minor or fragmentary architectural remains in Bristol – some tombs, a few fireplaces salvaged from long-demolished houses, and one relatively minor building, the Red Lodge, originally in the garden of a larger house.

It was built between 1577 and '85 by Sir John Younge, the Collector of Customs in Bristol.* One of the more prosperous Bristolians of his time, he had built his main residence on the site of the old Carmelite Monastery which he had demolished. His Great House was in turn demolished in 1863 to make way for the Colston Hall. It seems that he used Red Lodge's main room for his function as a magistrate, and the arcaded garden front (now glazed-in) to allow views over his garden, his Great House and the ships in the Frome below. The exterior was transformed early in the eighteenth century when the casement windows were replaced by sashes, and the gables removed and replaced by the present heavy cornice. Much more recently the original render and red lime-wash was hacked off to expose rough stonework never intended to be seen. It is time the render and colour were replaced, even if the gables and open arcade cannot be.

The interiors, restored by the City Art Gallery when it acquired the house in 1948, are of some importance. The fine stair with its barley-sugar banisters dates from the early eighteenth century, but several rooms survive from Sir John Younge's time. The finest, the Great Oak Room, is, as usual, on the first floor. Entirely original apart from the sash windows, it is an apartment of great magnificence, entered through a slightly later internal porch. Such porches were fairly common at this date, installed to reduce the draughts which, bearing in mind the huge fires and colossal flues, must have been tempestuous. The upper part of the porch contains the arms of Sir John and his wife, supported by figures among which are Red Indians, alluding to Bristol's trade with America. The room itself contains some of the richest oak panelling in England, and an enormous and elaborate two-storey chimney piece containing another coat of Younge's arms, and figures of Hope, Charity, Prudence and Justice, referring to Younge's role as an alderman (i.e. magistrate) and therefore suggesting the room's main

use. The plaster ceiling is divided into compartments by intersecting straps which drop down as pendants. It must surely be original, but its design pays no regard to the shape of the room or the fireplace projecting into it. Other rooms, only slightly less magnificent, survive from Younge's time. This was a minor lodge; what must the interiors of the Great House have been like?

In 1854 the widow of the wicked Lord Byron bought the Red Lodge so that Mary Carpenter, Bristol pioneer of Ragged Schools and builder of the first reformatory in the city, could use it as a second reformatory.

* The monument to Younge and his wife Dame Joan Wadham is in the Cathedral. She survived him by 17 years and, as was usual at that time, almost certainly had it made during her lifetime to ensure that it gave the information she wanted. The only effigy on the monument, which the inscription makes clear is to both of them, is of her, in full size and in colour, with her coat of arms emblazoned above. We are shown what she and her favourite dress looked like, told about her first husband, given a list of her children by both men, and, never to be forgotten, the name and title of her aristocratic father. But we are told scarcely anything about the less well-born Sir John, not even the date of his death. The Dame had lost interest in him. At what long-forgotten marital drama does this seldom-visited monument hint?

St Michael's Hill and Christmas Steps ★★★★

St Michael's Hill and Christmas Steps are a route as old as Bristol itself: the start of the very ancient trackway leading out of Bristol to the north. When the town's first circuit of walls were built at some unknown date in the eleventh or twelfth centuries, the way north started at what became St John's Gate, and went along the short length of Christmas Street to Frome Bridge. Pedestrians, if they could face the mud and the climb, then went up what is now Christmas Steps. That was always too steep for wagons, so they had to turn left onto Host Street and then right onto Steep (now Colston) Street to reach the bottom of what is now St Michael's Hill.

The great width of St Michael's Hill almost certainly arose because being steep and undoubtedly muddy throughout its early years, the way got wider and wider as vehicles left the track to find less rutted routes on either side. (Even in the eighteenth century many stretches of road in England grew to several hundred yards in width for this reason.) As the first timber-and-thatch houses began to be built on each side they were set back from the ever-widening thoroughfare. Over the years they were demolished as they became decrepit, were rebuilt on the same plot, and in many cases doubt-less demolished and rebuilt again. Those we see today are a glorious confusion dating from every century since the seventeenth, and exhibiting most of the architectural fashions of those years.

It is not known when St Michael's church was founded, but it is known that an earlier church on the same site was in existence by 1193, so this early extra-mural suburb must have existed well before then for it to serve. The present church is a rebuilding of 1775-7. The nunnery of St Mary Magdalen, which faced it across the road, was demolished some time after its dissolution in about 1539. The loutish concrete hospital at the top, which elbows itself into the hitherto continuous succession of

small-scale narrow frontages, is a reminder that St Michael's Hill is now the border between two huge and ruthless empires, the University on the west and the BRI on the east. Both, in the interest of what they consider to be greater needs, have shown themselves to be heedless of 'unimportant' historic buildings which stand in their way. Despite that, St Michael's Hill remains the most picturesque of Bristol's streets. It is worth briefly examining why that is. It is because being curved there is always something hidden out of sight, but about to come into view as one moves up or down. It is due to the mixture of sizes, architectural styles, flat parapets and steep gables, to the dozens of building materials, colours and textures, to the pavements that run beside the carriageway and then climb up to look down upon it, to the frontages undulating in and out, to the fact that they are continuous and where there is a gap there is something worthwhile – Colston's Almshouse (q.v.) – to look at, and above all, to the glorious view over the city as one comes down the hill.

Christmas Steps remained narrow because it didn't have to suffer vehicles seeking a less rutted surface. It was not paved and given steps at the top until 1669. Before then, in the sixteenth century, it had become the cutlers' quarter and was called Knifesmiths' Street; in 1669 it was renamed Queen Street Steps, as a political gesture to the new Royal government. I don't know when the present name was adopted but it appears to have been at about the time when the Chapel of the Three Kings of Cologne, part of Foster's Almshouse at the top (q.v.), was restored in 1883.

Christmas Steps is one of the city's few remaining ancient lanes, and of those that survive has the most strongly medieval character, although the fronts of the houses all date from the eighteenth or nineteenth century. This character depends on the fact that the lane is steep and tightly enclosed on either side and, crucially, at the bottom, where it is crossed by the almost equally ancient thoroughfare of Host Street. In the 1960s this was shattered when the attractively ramshackle house which closed the view at the bottom was demolished to create the Inner Ring Road. The view looking down suddenly became dominated by roaring traffic. In 1975, when my practice was commissioned by Bristol Municipal Charities to sort out Host Street and the adjacent medieval St Bartholomew's Hospital, we proposed to put a new building at the bottom of Christmas Steps to re-close the view. I was subjected to the usual barrage of criticism when the plans were published but have heard no complaints since it was built. The complex of lanes and the sense of narrow enclosure was thus regained and extended.

Ashton Court ★★ Bower Ashton
fifteenth century, 1633, eighteenth century, 1803

The ancient deer park at Ashton is outside the scope of this book, but it deserves a brief mention. It was licensed in 1392 and sited as usual on mostly poor quality land, in this instance rising steeply up from the house. Many of its ancient pollard oaks survive and are said to be one of the finest collections in Britain.

The park with much surrounding farmland was bought in 1545 by the merchant Smyth family, who remained there for 401 years, until 1946. The medieval house they acquired was of substantial size, but over the years they added to it until it became what it is now, the largest of the country mansions that have come within the ambit of ever-expanding Bristol. I have never been able to love it. This is partly because since 1959 it has

absurdly attributed to the great Inigo Jones, the first classical architect in Britain. It does show his influence, though badly digested and not fully understood. The ground-floor windows have Jones's alternating triangular and curved pediments over them, the first-floor windows have flat cornices which – correctly – break forward over the console brackets which support them. The attic windows are oval. All well and good, but everything else is wrong. The proportions of the windows are not quite right; the console brackets over the first-floor windows have absurd ornament carved into them; the parapet on the roof (a Jonesian must) is actually carved with the Jacobean ornament that Jones had reacted against. On their own these solecisms, as Jones would

been owned by Bristol Corporation, and suffers from municipal philistinism – imagine what it would be like if the National Trust had owned it for 50 years.

The earliest and most attractive part of the house is the west-facing entrance front and the bits and pieces that can be seen over it. It was built in the fifteenth century and a few original fragments are still recognisable, but it was much altered in the eighteenth century – the porch, for example, dates from around 1800. Entered from the porch is the Great Hall, also altered at various dates, with a heavily repaired but authentic fifteenth-century timber roof.

The long south-facing west wing is contemporary with the Great Hall, but in about 1633 it was modernised and given the external facing we see today. It has often been

have considered them, don't give offence today. But something else does.

The name of the designer (probably a mason) is unknown, but whoever he was had an extremely difficult problem to solve, and it defeated him. He had been brought up in the medieval tradition, and as the Victorian Gothicists loved to point out, medieval architecture gave designers the freedom to place windows and other features where they were needed, and not where the regularity of a classical façade dictated. The problem facing Thomas Smyth's mason-architect was that he had to fit a regular façade onto an existing set of rooms which were not regular. No doubt he found that where he wanted to put a window there was either a wall in the way or it was off-centre in a room he wanted to be symmetrical. Plenty of architects since him have had to face the same problem and the better ones have always found ways around it. Smyth's designer didn't. At first glance it seems that he did, by arranging the windows symmetrically in groups of 5-3-5. One soon notices that this is not so, they are arranged 3-2-3-3-2. One then becomes aware that even this is not exact and that the intervals between the windows vary a great deal, totally without order. It is like hearing someone whistling a well-known tune and constantly, but inconsistently, getting the time wrong. It is very unpleasant.

The façade, nonetheless, was advanced for this still architecturally backward part of the West Country, but at some date in the nineteenth century it was badly damaged when the oak mullions and transoms were removed from the windows and replaced by sashes with great staring panes of plate glass. Before then, just after 1800, the situation had been made worse when the family decided to demolish the stables and build an east wing to balance the west one, and to renovate and heighten the gatehouse between them to form the central focus of a long symmetrical composition. But what resulted isn't symmetrical; the wings aren't even the same length, and the huge Gothic windows are set at different levels. Nothing balances. If the cross-mullioned windows could be re-instated, the western portion of the south façade would be improved, but the disturbing arrangement of the windows would remain, and the entire façade would still be an offence.

King Street ★★★★
1650s, 1660s and later

It is instructive to compare the character of Bristol's streets with those of Bath. All the notable Bath streets are classical, that is, each building surrenders its individuality to the greater whole.

In Bristol's most notable streets (but not Clifton's) each building is allowed to express itself, to be big or small, loud or quiet. Bath is, or rather was, essentially aristocratic. Its streets express order and discipline. Bristol was mercantile and its streets express freedom and competition. As King Street, St Michael's Hill and Old Market demonstrate, varied streets can be just as attractive as classical ones: neither is 'better' than the other – though the classical ones are always considered to be posher.

In 1650 a row of houses was built along the outer face of the city wall which had been built in the 1240s across the peninsula formed by the diversion of the Frome. (A bastion of the wall can still be seen in the yard behind St Nicholas's Almshouses.) The confidence following the restoration of Charles II encouraged speculators to take up leases from the Corporation to build a further row, to form the other side of what was tactfully given the name King Street. (Bristol had changed sides embarrassingly often in the Civil War, and needed to demonstrate loyalty to the new government.) By then classical, uniform, streets had begun to appear in London, and they prompted Bristol Corporation to require uniformity in the King Street houses. But this was Bristol, and what uniformity resulted was no more than what economy dictated in any case: the houses were almost as narrow and cramped as those in the central city, and of the same timber construction because that was the cheapest way to build. The two sides of the street are not parallel, or even straight, the plots are far from regular, and no two houses were identical. In the result there can't have been much more regularity than in any other Bristol street at that time, except the height of the houses, all of which had three storeys and attics in their gabled roofs. But if the houses were cramped, the street was not. It was gloriously, wonderfully, wide open to the air and the sun, free from the city stinks and clatter.

For many years numbers 7 and 8, two typical King Street houses, were my offices. Work on them revealed how they were built. Like all the houses in the street they

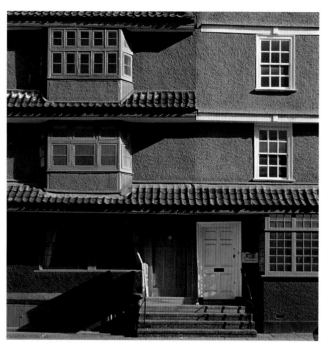

Numbers 7 and 8 King Street

were constructed on leases of three lives, i.e. for three generations, a period of perhaps 50 to 75 years. (Lessees sometimes put their lease in the name of one of their children, but high child mortality could make that a bad gamble.) This was an incentive to cut costs and build houses with a life expectancy of not much more than that, which is certainly what happened at 7 and 8, despite the fact that they have survived for 350 years. The two were built as one contract by the 'undertaker', who would have been a carpenter.* The setting-out of the cellars was highly incompetent, neither of them has a single right angle, and therefore the houses above them don't have one either. The party walls to numbers 6 and 9 are built of stone, as are all the cellar walls, but everything else is of oak, then the relatively cheap standard building timber. The method of erection of the ground and upper floors was to mortice the main upright posts, spaced about 8 feet apart, into wall plates at their bottom, and into heads laid over their tops. These heads support the posts of the walls above and the beams, which in turn carry the floor joists, and so on up to the attics. The partitions therefore consist of uprights and horizontals forming, very roughly, 8-foot squares. At this

* Undertakers of building contracts were often carpenters, and if they weren't they employed carpenters and joiners. They therefore made the coffins. In the nineteenth century some joiners began to specialise in this lugubrious trade and retained the term undertaker. To differentiate themselves, builders called themselves building contractors.

stage the framework lacked any stability except that given by the joints, which was sufficient only to hold everything together during construction. Stability was to be provided by diagonal bracing between the main posts. At this point the carpenter began to economise. He bought second-hand timbers from a ship which was being broken up. The ship, quite possibly one of the trows which traded between Welsh Back and the Wye valley, must have been quite small because most of the timbers are curved, and none of them long enough to span diagonally from corner to corner of the frames. Instead they were placed as near opposite corners as possible, sometimes a long way from the desirable position. As a result the frames were not properly triangulated, and to some extent were not fully stable. The partitions were completed by the insertion of vertical studs at about 14 inches spacing. These also were curved ships' timbers which, when they were uncovered, presented an incredibly gimcrack appearance. They bristled with ancient iron nails, were cut away by ancient joints, and were drilled to take the trenails (wooden dowels used in shipbuilding, pronounced trennels) which had once fixed the ship's boarding. Most of them, all charred for preservation, were still in position. When all these studs were in place, both faces of the partitions were covered with riven oak laths, the interstices of which gave a key to the plaster which was bound with cow hair. Once again second-hand materials had been used – many of the laths were old barrel staves. That was not all. When the yard at the back was excavated, the foundations of an old wall were uncovered. Most of its stones were obviously local, but some were large pebbles of a sort never found naturally in Bristol. They were presumably brought to the city as ship's ballast, discarded nearby and re-cycled by the builder. The fact that these houses still stand, though warped, twisted and settled, and still provide excellent accommodation, is a remarkable testimony to timber-frame construction, and above all, to that superlative building material, English oak. (It's no myth: imported oak is inferior.)

Since the building of the original houses, the street has been in constant change, becoming more varied, almost always for the better. At first it was occupied by families from the upper strata of the merchant traders. (Bristol, unlike other provincial capitals, has never had any aristocrats' town houses.) The traders lived on their upper floors and used the ground floors for their businesses.

Kitchens and other offices were in the yards at the back, and the cellars, half below ground and half above, were used to store merchandise. The cellars were accessible by the house's staircase, but in most cases also from the street so that goods could be taken in and out. In number 7 the street access survives, consisting of a low removable wooden panel in its front wall, hinged flaps in the pavement, and steps flanked by stone kerbs down which barrels could be rolled the few feet into the cellar.

King Street was Bristol's best address for half a century or so, until Queen Square and Prince Street were built. From then onwards it slipped, slowly but inexorably, down the social scale. The building of the Coopers' Hall (q.v.) in the 1740s may have arrested the decline for a while, but the Coopers' Company itself was in terminal decline. Even so, many houses remained residential until well into the twentieth century, although from the mid-nineteenth century they had begun to be replaced by

brick warehouses and workshops. The Theatre Royal (q.v.), which for its first century and a half was entered from a narrow lane between two houses, made no impact on the street until it was given a King Street front at the beginning of the twentieth century, by which time it had itself slipped down the social scale, from the trough of which it was rescued in 1942. In 1970 the Coopers' Hall became its grand entrance foyer. The street is now crammed with restaurants and pubs.

King Street is an object lesson in the pleasures of urban variety – of building materials, colours, architectural styles and, above all, of different scales. All three floors of St Nicholas's Almshouses, gables and all, could fit into the first floor of the Coopers' Hall, for (an admittedly extreme but glorious) example.

The Llandoger Trow ★★★ King Street
1664

The Llandoger Trow has been an inn since at least the 1760s. (A trow was a flat-bottomed sailing barge used for river traffic, and it is on record in the eighteenth century that several trows involved in trade with Wales berthed at Welsh Back.) The inn was the westernmost of a group of five more or less identical houses, of which the two at the eastern end were destroyed in the blitz of the winter 1940-41. In 1962 the inn and its two neighbours were bought by Berni Inns, one of the early pub/restaurant chains, and converted into a single building. At that time the ethics of dealing with old buildings were in their infancy and the conversion left much to be desired. It is now hard to know what of the interior is original, what is fake and what has been brought into the building from elsewhere. Most of the panelling is probably original, as are the stairs, a fireplace which is surprisingly gothic and surviving bits of decorative plasterwork in the ceilings. The black painted ceiling in the front bar is also original.

Bernis tidied up the exterior slightly, particularly at street level by removing some of the hinged panels which gave access to the cellars. Apart from that the exterior survives in fair condition, by far the best of the timber houses to survive from a city in which, until the eighteenth century, almost all houses were timber-framed and gabled. It seems that all those which do survive in Bristol date from the seventeenth century, though it is hard to be certain because timber construction changed very slowly over the centuries. In these houses one little decorative detail could not be much earlier than the 1660s – the typically renaissance arch in the windows. Of course many changes took place long before Bernis bought the houses. In about 1700 several of the original casement windows were replaced by the newly fashionable sliding sashes, all of them much too horizontal in proportion to slide without racking. Joiners were slow to realise that vertically proportioned sashes slide much more easily.

The biggest change in the appearance of the houses probably took place soon after 1868 (when a photograph of the houses in the Reece Winstone Collection was taken). Before that period exposed oak timbers were left in their beautiful silvery colour. Then, when a permanent black paint distilled from tar became available, it became fashionable, particularly in the west of England, to blacken them. Today, this aesthetic vandalism is accepted as the norm, and the majority of people believe that timber buildings were always 'black and white'. It will be many years before it is accepted that they look far more beautiful when the oak has its natural weathered colour.

Colston's Almshouse ★★★ St Michael's Hill
1691

In the entry on St Stephen's church (page 25), mention was made of Bristol's remarkably few medieval parish churches compared to other towns of comparable size. But though it lagged far behind other British cities in that respect, Bristol led them all in the foundation of charitable institutions. By the eighteenth century there were four boys' schools, one girls' school, the first workhouse in Britain, the country's second public library and numerous almshouses. Some of these services had previously been provided by the monasteries: in Bristol more than other places the laity took over and surpassed what the monks had provided. Even the suppression of the chantries found a successor, because to some degree almshouses took over their purpose, the almsmen and women being required to pray for the soul of the founder. In addition they had a more immediate motive, though doubtless not the main one: founders and their families, sometimes in perpetuity, had the right to nominate their retired servants or poor relations to places in the almshouse.

Almshouses came in all shapes, but the favourite, as here, was the quadrangle (as it still is for old people's flats, to gain the same advantages of peace, seclusion and community). Colston's was built in 1691 around three sides of a quadrangle, with a chapel in the middle of the central range. Each little house has its own front door, and the lower windows have alternating pediments. The houses are beautifully tied together, both visually and socially, by the double-height chapel to which the eye is drawn by its pediment and tiny bell cupola, but also, almost mesmerically, by the two oval windows and the circular clock face above them.

To a visitor of the twenty-first century one of the most instructive things about this delightful building is its windows, all of which still have their original stone cross mullions and transoms. Until about 1700 all houses had windows of this type. They are now very rare because after 1700 fashion dictated that they should be replaced by the newly invented sliding sashes. Fortunately, frugal trustees of charities rarely bowed to expensive fashions in administering their charges.

Colston's Almshouse is an enchantment, still, after three centuries, fulfilling the function for which Edward Colston saw the need.

Queen Square ★★★★
1699 onwards

The corporate finances, which had been shaky until revenue from the development of King Street began to improve things, decided the Corporation in 1699 to build Queen Square and Prince Street on the rest of the promontory between the Avon and the Frome. In Queen Square they wanted to achieve a more up-to-date uniformity than had been obtained in King Street, and to follow where Inigo Jones's Covent Garden had led nearly three-quarters of a century earlier, so the building leases carefully specified in detail how the façades were to be designed. But the City Surveyor who had to enforce this clearly had a wife and large family to feed which the builders generously recognised. So things didn't work out quite as the Councillors had intended. The houses did all have brick façades with stone quoins, timber sashes and, very approximately, level parapets and roof lines, but within this overall discipline the façades varied enormously. As in King Street, most of the houses had substantial outhouses in their gardens, some of which had their occupants' business frontages on the roads at the back. Leases were taken up slowly so the last house was not finished until 1727. Despite the failure to achieve uniformity it was a remarkable achievement which, surprisingly, historians have not hitherto recognised: it was the first residential square to be built in England outside London (though Scotland had an earlier example in the now long-demolished Milne's Square in Edinburgh of 1684).

Until the houses in the Square began to become available, everybody except those living in King Street lived in the city's narrow crowded streets where freely roaming pigs were still employed to recycle the stinking filth. All but a tiny handful of the grandest houses were timber-framed, narrow and cramped. Queen Square, quickly followed by the now lost St James's Square, brought about what, without any exaggeration, was the most profound revolution ever to occur in Bristol's housing. The broad brick façades, the sash windows, the grass and the trees, at last made Bristolians recognise that – if they could afford it – they too could live like the more comfortably off in London and Paris. From then onwards there was a constant migration away from the

old city within the walls. The thousand or so years of timber house building in Bristol had finished. (But not for ever. Timber is still the cheapest building material and it is fascinating to see how, when allied with modern scientific knowledge, it is now in use for house building again.)

Two houses in the south side are worth looking at carefully. Number 36, of about 1700, (opposite, right) is one of the earliest houses to survive. Its façade retains all its original features, such as the timber modillion cornice and the sashes set flush with the face of the wall, both of which went out of use in Bristol a few years after the London Building Act of 1707 made them illegal there

as a fire risk. Only the original thick glazing bars in the sashes are missing; they were replaced by the present thin ones later in the same century or early in the next. Number 29, of 1709-11, (opposite, left) is the richest of the original façades to survive. The mason who built it knew that Doric, Ionic and Corinthian columns should be used in that order up the façade, but he clearly didn't know why; nor did he know that his pediments should be supported on entablatures, and not appear to balance on the key-stones in the flat arches over the windows. As classical architecture the façade is absurd, but we can now enjoy its naive charm.

By the time the Square was completed in 1727 there had been a revolution in taste in Bristol. Somebody with authority and influence must have known that the great squares in Paris were adorned with bronze equestrian statues of the king. In 1729 Michael Rysbrack's figure of Edward Colston in All Saints' church (q.v.) revealed his genius to everybody in Bristol, so about three years later he and Scheemakers were invited to submit competitive models for an equestrian figure of William III to be set in the Square. The Council chose much the better of the two and commissioned Rysbrack. His statue has been accepted as the finest equestrian figure in Britain ever since. (Scheemakers was commissioned by Hull's Corporation, where his statue also survives to this day.)

The destruction of the north and west sides of the

Square in the devastating and bloody riots of 1831, and the later destruction of houses here and there on the other sides, did little to disturb what uniformity there was, because with few exceptions all the gaps were filled with buildings which approximately maintained the original near-uniformity of height. The biggest change was that the more expensive, and therefore more fashionable, Bath stone replaced brick as a facing.

Queen Square remained Bristol's best address for a long time, housing most of the city's more prominent families, as well as the Lord Mayor's Mansion until it was burnt in the riots. The Square's social position began to slip only when the most prosperous merchants began to move out of the city altogether, most of them to Clifton

and a few other suburbs such as Frenchay, and the richest of them, such as the Elton family, to houses in the country where they became land-owning members of the squirearchy. By the 1840s the Square was no longer fashionable. All the poshest notables had left, too many of the houses had become tenements, and the architecture had gone into the state of low esteem which, for a few generations, is the inevitable fate of all buildings in all periods. Like 1960s buildings today it had become contemptible. In 1862 the Bristol and Clifton Railway Bill took advantage of the low property values to propose the demolition of the southern side of the Square to allow a line elevated on a viaduct to run along

its site, with a station facing south onto the Grove and north onto the Square. The Bill was defeated, but not because of the damage it would do to the Square – scarcely anybody objected to that. During this period of low esteem which lasted until well into the twentieth century, many houses were demolished to make way for warehouses and offices such as the Port Authority's headquarters, which paid scant respect, or none at all, to previous uniformities. Even so, a few houses continued to be lived in, until by the 1960s the only residents left were a few caretakers living on top floors.

The worst destruction since the riots took place in the 1930s when the north-west and south-east corners were demolished to make way for the new Redcliffe Way. The removal of the road has partially corrected that, but the yawning gap at the north-west corner remains, probably for ever, because unfortunate recent decisions by the city planners have allowed the creation of rights of light which will prevent building in the gap.

Queen Square is not an *architectural* ensemble of great beauty. It is, and always has been, too big for the houses to make the point which Inigo Jones's taller houses made in the much smaller Covent Garden. In addition, its buildings, even from the beginning, have always been too heterogeneous to make a satisfactory unity. It is, however, an urban space of great beauty. The trees form an attractive enclosure, being higher than the houses and enclosing a smaller area. Queen Square was a quite extraordinary achievement: it was the first English square outside London; and unlike its precursor, Covent Garden, it had the focus of an equestrian statue high on its plinth in its centre. The Square put Bristol at the forefront of English urban design until John Wood achieved that status for Bath.

Kings Weston House ★★★★★

Kings Weston Lane
1710-1719, 1763-8

In the seventeenth century Kings Weston was a country estate several miles from Bristol, with a Tudor house owned by one of the city's merchants (as were most of the large houses within 10 or 15 miles of Bristol). In 1679 the estate was bought by Sir Robert Southwell, and in 1710 his son, the Secretary of State for Ireland, Sir Edward Southwell, instructed the architect John Vanbrugh to knock all or most of it down and build anew.

Vanbrugh then was 45, four years away from his knighthood. Nobody has ever had so remarkable a career before taking up the practice of architecture. His contemporary, Christopher Wren, almost rivalled him in this respect, having started as a boy mathematical prodigy, then becoming an anatomist and professor of astronomy before taking up architecture. Vanbrugh had been a soldier, probably a spy for the Prince of Orange (the future William III), for which he spent four years in French prisons (including the Bastille), a herald and Clarenceaux King of Arms, a theatre owner, and what made him hugely famous, a playwright of witty and thoroughly bawdy plays which still fill theatres today. Then he became an architect. Unlike most architects, who have to start with a couple of small houses, he started with a couple of palaces, Castle Howard and Blenheim. Swift was as bemused as everyone: 'Van's genius, without thought or lecture, is hugely turn'd to architecture.'

Kings Weston, one of his smallest houses, stands tall and four-square, a block without flanking wings or any of the other devices which tie a house into the landscape. Two of its faces were altered 40 years after they were built, but two survive as he designed them: the entrance front facing west and the garden front facing south. Both are extremely severe with hardly any ornament, utterly unlike Vanbrugh's palaces. Poor Southwell protested at having this experiment in architectural minimalism thrust upon him, but Vanbrugh had his way. He usually did. The feature which transforms everything is on the roof, which is crowned by the tall chimney stacks joined together by arches into a sort of open temple: a little building sitting on a bigger one. Because only two sides of the house are now as Vanbrugh intended, it is best seen today as one moves around the south and west sides. There it can be seen as a dynamic cluster of planes, a dream castle, and Vanbrugh particularly loved what he called the 'castle air' of such Romantic block-like houses as Worksop and Wollaton.

Vanbrugh's interiors at Kings Weston have all been altered, but it is worth understanding the bones of what he created. The house consisted of rooms arranged around two huge halls: a two-storey entrance saloon, and behind it a three-storey stair hall. The wall between them was pierced by arches to allow views through from one to the other. When spectators in the saloon looked towards the arches they would have seen into and through a complex succession of spaces: first the huge one in which they stood; then the constriction of the arch; and beyond that the further constriction of one of the arches in the stone cage which supported the stair. Through that they would have glimpsed the biggest space of all, the huge stair hall. This static view would have been fascinating enough, but it would have been puzzling, impossible to comprehend until one moved to reveal more in order to understand what was going on. As with the exterior, Vanbrugh relied on movement: his design was kinetic. Probably few people at the time understood what he had created, certainly not the Southwell family who ruined it all in the 1760s when they made Vanbrugh's admittedly inconvenient house more usable. If only the interiors had survived into the twentieth century! – the age of the movies, the era that has discovered the thrill of Bristol Cathedral's spatial gymnastics. The Cathedral's master mason and Vanbrugh were similar sorts of genius.

If one can forget what was lost one can still enjoy the entrance saloon today. In the 1760s the Southwells inherited a large collection of family portraits (some rather dismal, some first-rate) and instructed the architect Robert Mylne to alter the saloon to display them. He filled in the arches and designed a series of plaster frames to hold the portraits. The resulting room, with its splendid chimney piece and marble floor, is extremely pleasant. Some of the smaller rooms, also modernised by Mylne, are worth seeing. The house generally, however, now seems slightly sad, not loved enough or appreciated for what it is.

Beside the short drive into the house is Vanbrugh's brewhouse, a building that could have been designed by nobody but him. The arched doorway with an exaggeratedly huge keystone over it, and above it the lunette window with a cill projecting so far forward as to be

almost a balcony, are typical of him. But the brewhouse's historically fascinating detail is the imitation machicolated parapet. Machicolation is one of several medieval forms that fascinated Vanbrugh, and it makes this little building an early example of what was soon to become the Gothic revival. The other garden buildings are, almost certainly, also by him.

Vanbrugh was a man of his time, as his great worldly success demonstrates, but he was also a man before his time: one of the three or four greatest architects Britain has produced.

Merchant Tailors' Almshouse ★★

Merchant Street in Broadmead

1701 Now a café

Well back in the medieval period the Merchant Tailors Company had established in Marsh Street a hospital (meaning an almshouse) for members who had fallen on hard times. In 1701 they built this more convenient replacement. Like Colston's Almshouse of 10 years earlier (q.v.) it is built around three sides of a quadrangle, but it is much smaller and has no chapel. Also like Colston's Almshouse, but unlike the vast majority of seventeenth-century buildings, it still retains its cross mullioned windows (which in 1701 were beginning to look old-fashioned as the new sashes began to appear everywhere), but it has other features which were distinctly up to date. It has a hipped roof, a modillioned cornice, and long and short stone quoins at the angles of the walls. [A modillioned cornice is one supported on little square brackets, and quoins are large blocks of ashlar stone used to reinforce the corners of buildings, which at that time were considered to need such visual strengthening.] These two features mark the great change which took place in Bristol's domestic architecture at the turn of the seventeenth into the eighteenth century with the building of Queen Square (q.v.).

The interior of the almshouse has been destroyed, which is a pity, but the surviving front has been given an extraordinary new use. It is set, like a large porch, in front of the huge Galleries shopping complex, which at this point has been very carefully designed to focus down upon it. No doubt some people are horrified at the juxtaposition of a tiny eighteenth-century building and a huge modern glass complex, but the Gallery's architect, Leslie Jones, has carried it off with such wit and verve that it is a minor if slightly flashy triumph.

Bishopsworth Manor House ★★

Church Road, Bishopsworth

1720s

Kings Weston House was too severe to find imitators in Bristol, where people who could afford to build wanted more show for their money. But it does have one tiny and out-of-the-way follower, Bishopsworth Manor House. Once set in its ancestral fields, it now sits, not too unhappily, in the suburbia which has swallowed them. It's a very curious little building, in fact not far up from a farmhouse, but with just sufficient distinguishing marks of rank to set it apart. It has the essential pediment, though very small, over a slightly projecting entrance bay, and a quite decent doorway with a projecting hood. The tall chimney stacks (some of which are dummies) are joined into a square arcade sitting on the high pantiled roof in a hopeful imitation of Vanbrugh's at Kings Weston House on the other side of Bristol. The house dates from the 1720s, soon after Kings Weston was complete.

Apart from its small size, the main reason why this manor house looks a bit like a farmhouse is that it is built of the local lias, a cheap, cold grey stone which is too hard to be cut into smooth ashlar blocks and has to be used as rubble. It is perhaps the least attractive of English building stones, and therefore used only in cottages and farmhouses, never in grand dwellings.

And yet this house has an undeniable charm, naive and unsophisticated though it is. Its designer, probably the local mason, didn't quite know how to design all the status symbols he had been instructed to incorporate. The tiny pediment is too steep for classical correctness, the chimney arcade is dinky rather than lordly, and the highly visible hipped roof was unfashionable in the 1720s when roofs were hidden behind parapets. Despite all that, the house stands tall and erect on its dignity. Today, behind its wall and modest gate piers, it retains just enough ground (it seems impertinent to call it a front garden), and just enough trees and outbuildings to support its manorial pride.

Bishops' House **** Clifton Hill
1711

The medieval Bishops' Palace (originally the Abbots') was burnt by rioters in 1831 and its successor on Redland Green was burnt by German bombs in 1940. Ignoring these fiery portents the Diocese bought this house backing onto the old parish churchyard on Clifton Hill. Again the stay was not to last: the bishops have recently been driven out again, this time by finance, not flames. Now back in private hands the house's façade has been cleaned and tidied up. It looks splendid, though almost hidden from view behind a high hedge. Fortunately it can still be seen if you peer over the gate. Be nosy, don't miss it.

It is convenient for historians that the house is dated 1711 in its pediment, because, until you study it with some care, it looks a decade or two later. Its designer is unknown, but George Townesend, who designed and built the lovely tower of All Saints' in Corn Street (q.v.), is the most probable candidate.

The façade of creamy Bath stone is beautifully balanced, very restrained and classical, in its simple way perfect. I use those words advisedly. The best definition of classical beauty is Alberti's paraphrase of the ancient Roman architect Vitruvius: beauty is 'the harmony and concord of all the parts achieved in such a way that nothing can be added or taken away or altered except for the worse.' Vitruvius was applying to architecture Aristotle's rule that in poetry 'the structural union of the parts should be such that if any one of them is displaced or removed, the whole will be disjointed and disturbed.' It would be hard to find a façade that better illustrates this golden rule. It is therefore worthwhile to analyse it to try to find where this elusive classical beauty lies.

The core of the design is the centrepiece, slightly projecting in front of the side bays. It consists of the doorway and a window, set in stonework with its horizontal joints emphasised by being cut in a V shape. In the Palladian buildings of the next few decades in England it was usual, almost a cliché, to use rustication right across the ground storey, providing a base upon which the upper floor or floors could sit. Townesend – I have persuaded myself it was he – used this horizontal device to emphasise his vertical feature, something the Palladians scarcely ever did. I don't suppose many people notice this contradiction, but the slight *frisson* it generates explains a great deal of this façade's appeal: a *frisson* strictly controlled because it is achieved so quietly and modestly. The doorway is simply a pair of pilasters supporting a heavy entablature and a segmental pediment. Above it the narrow window and its tiny triangular pediment pointing upwards are another contribution to the verticality of the centrepiece. It is beautifully balanced on either side by the slightly recessed side wings with their plain unemphasised stonework and segmental headed windows. The balustrade on the roof and its vases survive intact (and again look later than 1711). Perfect? I really think that in its way it is. What could be added or taken away or altered without spoiling this beautifully harmonious façade?

All Saints' ★★★★ Corn Street

eleventh century, fifteenth century, 1712
Redundant. Now diocesan offices

The High Street, running up from the bridge, was insignificant little Bricgstow's earliest street. The town grew up around its junction with Wine, Corn and Broad Streets. Their crossing was marked by churches on three of the four corners, the long lost St Ewen's, Christ Church (q.v.) and All Saints'. The first mention of All Saints' in a document was in 1153, but it was almost certainly founded long before that.

In the early fifteenth century the Norman nave and aisles were rebuilt, but the two western bays had to remain because rooms (which survive) had been built over their aisles, so some interesting Norman work remains. The aisles of the three bays which were rebuilt are as high as the nave, which makes this what is now called a hall church. They are common in Germany but rare in England. The most famous English example is Bristol Cathedral, which possibly gave the unknown designer of All Saints' the idea. He produced a most delightful interior, well worth seeing if you can talk your way in.

The church contains the 1729 monument to Edward Colston, designed by the great James Gibbs, architect of St Martin-in-the-Fields in Trafalgar Square and many other famous buildings. The figure of Colston was carved by the equally great but then young and unknown Michael Rysbrack. His work here was noted and three years later he was one of the two sculptors chosen for the competition which won him the commission for the superlative Queen Square statue of William III.

Externally the church's three Perpendicular windows facing onto Corn Street are a pleasant contrast to the adjoining classical buildings, but the glory is the tower – a glory and a triumph, because its history was utterly unpromising. The medieval tower was demolished in 1712 and then a succession of three masons worked on the new one, each with different ideas. The result is that the tower starts as classical, then becomes Gothic and finally reverts for most of its height to classical again. That's not all: in 1807 the splendid baroque cupola displeased the obscure District Surveyor who was asked to look at some defects in it, so he pulled it down and built the surviving decent but duller one. If the product of this committee who never met together is a camel, it's a compliment to those unfortunate creatures. The

mason who designed the original cupola and the classical top two-thirds of the tower, was George Townesend, who died young at the age of 38. Apart from a couple of monuments in Long Ashton church nothing else of his is known. Nonetheless, some fine buildings in Bristol must be by him. (See the entry on Bishops' House.) His All Saints' tower is a superb ornament to Bristol's most architecturally glorious street.

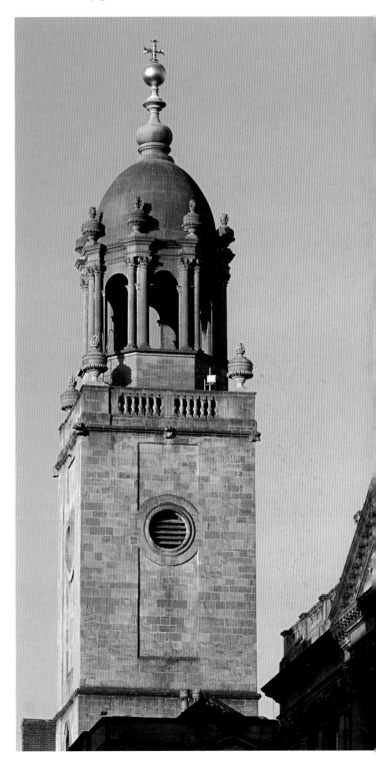

Orchard Street ★★★

1718-22

The entry on King Street commented on the difference between Bath's most notable streets, which are classical, each house surrendering its individuality to the greater whole, and Bristol's, which are picturesque, each house expressing its individuality. Orchard Street is Bristol's most notable classical street, and it pre-dates Bath's.

By 1716 most of the plots in Queen Square had been taken and built upon, and the ground leases in King Street were beginning to be renewed. Flushed with success – literally, it was notorious that a significant proportion of the corporate revenue was spent on sumptuous, frequent, and drunken dinners – the town councillors looked for more, and their corporate eyes settled on the orchard belonging to Queen Elizabeth's Hospital, which their predecessors had bought when the Hospital of St Mark was suppressed. They resolved to build a street of houses on the orchard. They could see that the requirement of uniformity in their previous leases had not produced the regularity which by then had become socially, and therefore financially, essential.

So this time the ground leases were much more specific: 'all houses built fronting the Street the front shall be built with brick all alike and the walls carried up above the Eves of the houses and no Mundillions or Coves shall be made.' [They were a known fire risk] 'That stone walls shall be made betwixt each house and all the other walls (except the front) to be of stone.' The heights and number of storeys are then laid down, and 'all the windows in the front of the houses shall be sash windows of an equal heighth', i.e. equal on each floor but graded in height upwards. (Some have been subsequently altered.) The width of the street was to be 30 feet, which before building was complete in 1722, was widened to 50 feet at the north end.

The result was what is now the most complete eighteenth-century street in Bristol. The Corporation, pursuing profit before beauty, had nonetheless produced an entirely satisfying environment. It was able to do so because the individual builders and their clients were prepared to accept a certain amount of uniformity, and the Corporation was prepared to accept a certain amount of individuality, but not enough to damage the over-all sense of order – some houses have individually designed doorways, one has carved keystones over its windows, and so on. The builders were free to design the interiors however they wished. Several houses have fine original features, for example no. 15, which has some lovely rococo plasterwork. Externally, two subsequent changes have damaged the concept. The first is relatively minor: the replacement in the windows of the original small panes and thick glazing bars by larger panes and thinner bars. The other is more serious: the painting of the façades. It has ruined the contrast between the brickwork and the stone lesenes between each house, and requires expensive re-painting every few years.

Dowry Square ★ Hotwells

1720-1750

The Square was laid out in about 1720 by the Bristol carpenter and surveyor George Tully, to take advantage of the growing number of people visiting the Hot Well. Although born in Surrey, Tully served his apprenticeship as a house carpenter in Bristol. He picked up a shrewd knowledge of building development from somewhere, and added to it a very real flair for design. In addition to Dowry Square he was responsible for some splendid buildings in Bristol – among them the Friends' Meeting House in the Friars (now the Brasserie Blanc) and, almost certainly, Wesley's Chapel in Broadmead (q.v.). In addition to his other talents he obviously had business acumen, because he died a comfortably wealthy man.

He planned Dowry Square to be open on its south side to allow sun in and views out to the river, and produced a controlling scheme whereby the central house in each of the three sides should be five windows wide, and those flanking them, three. For some reason plots were taken up slowly, the last going in 1750. As always when that happens, taste changed over the years and Tully had to allow modifications to his initial scheme, though all the houses were faced with red brick. Even that was breached later when many houses were stuccoed, and the Clifton Dispensary of 1823, built long after his death in 1770, was stone-faced. Like Queen Square, the result is a pleasant hotch potch rather than the ordered architectural composition he had had in mind. It doesn't matter now, because the trees in the central garden have become tall and make it impossible to see all of the Square in one view. Tully also designed the adjacent Chapel Row and the long lost Dowry Chapel (now the site of 1960s flats).

The Square has had some distinguished residents, amongst them Dr Beddoes, who in 1799 opened his famous Pneumatic Institution in number 6. Many of the outstanding literary characters of the time were his guests, including Coleridge, Southey and Maria Edgeworth. The subsequently knighted Humphry Davy was his assistant.

Eighteenth-century ironwork ★★★★

St Mary Redcliffe, St Stephen's and
the Lord Mayor's Chapel

The standard of craftsmanship in baroque Europe, when everything which was made was still handmade, is almost astounding to our eyes when we realise that craftsmen were not merely the executants but the designers of what they made. A considerable amount survives in Bristol, particularly in its churches, but a huge amount was destroyed in the following period of inevitable reaction against the work of the immediate past. Up to the middle of the twentieth century everything baroque was considered barbaric and in dreadful taste. To some small extent the decorative ironwork seems to have been exempt because its essentially baroque character was not recognised, but even so, much was destroyed in the eighteenth and nineteenth centuries as being far too frivolous for places of worship.

What survives in Bristol's churches is now rightly famous, largely due to the superbly gifted brothers, William and Simon Edney, smiths who were active in the years around 1700. It was the custom to keep the mayor's sword of state in his parish church during his period of office, and in order to display it with sufficient pomp each church had a wrought-iron rest fixed to a wall on which to hold it. Many have been lost, but perhaps the best example is in St Stephen's church, where it was placed after it was salvaged from St Nicholas's after it was bombed in the war. Considering that it is really no more than a metal bracket to hold a bit of old iron it is an extraordinarily fantastic object. Nowadays most new 'wrought iron' is just lengths of bent steel bar welded together in tediously repetitive S shapes: the sword rest is a confection of thick, thin and tapering iron bars, and swirling acanthus leaves hammered out of sheet into an inventive three-dimensional riot of shapes. There are other examples in St Mary Redcliffe and the Lord Mayor's Chapel (the latter salvaged from the bombed Temple church).

The churches also contain wonderful iron gates by the Edneys and others, for example a pair in the Lord Mayor's Chapel salvaged, like its sword rest, from the Temple church, and another in St Stephen's salvaged from St Nicholas's. The largest and most impressive are in St Mary Redcliffe (see facing page). They also are refugees, not from bombing but from changing taste. They are large fragments from the church's choir screen, which was made in 1710 by William Edney (for £110). Such transparent iron screens are frequently seen in central European churches but very rarely in England, where Protestant taste came to see them as too giddy and fanciful, not 'serious'. So St Mary Redcliffe's screen was removed in 1756 and its gates put in a less liturgically prominent place under the tower.

Redland Court ★★★ Redland Court Road

1735 Now Redland High School

The Redland estate was bought by John Cossins for his transformation from London merchant to country gentleman. His architect John Strahan demolished the Elizabethan house and built this new one, which was finished in 1735. 148 years later the land was sold for housing development and Redland High School bought the house. That saved it from imminent destruction, but at the price of unsuitable alterations and intrusive new classroom blocks. Amongst the alterations are the removal of the glazing bars from the windows and the

addition of horrible glass canopies at front and back, both of which have inflicted aesthetic damage out of all proportion to the ease with which they could be corrected.

The house, now far from the countryside, was intended to be the archetypal Palladian country house, and comes quite close to that ideal. Built on a raised platform probably surviving from the earlier house, it has the usual columned centrepiece with a pediment filled by Cossin's arms supported by putti, and a balustrade on the roof with stone vases. A pedantic examination, however, soon reveals Strahan's relaxed attitude to the Palladian rules, some of them unwritten, which had become absurdly tyrannical. He had been brought up in the much freer, rather baroque, era of Wren and Vanbrugh. But his grammatical errors and naughty proportions, which were so offensive to correct Palladians such as Lord Burlington and John Wood of Bath, are recognised by few people today and upset nobody.

Internally much original decoration survives. The best rooms are the three on the ground floor, with their plasterwork, fireplaces and panelling, the entrance hall and the two staircases.

The house is a treasure, but at the moment a faded and slightly sad one.

Redland Chapel ★★★★   Redland Green Road

1740-43

When John Cossins moved into his new house in 1735, his parish church was two miles away at Westbury-on-Trym, so in 1740 he commissioned his architect, John Strahan, to build a private chapel for his family and servants a few hundred yards uphill from the house. It was finished in 1743, but by then Strahan had died and another local architect, William Halfpenny, was engaged to supervise the completion of his design.

Strahan's Chapel reveals, even more than his house, his professional upbringing in the restrained English baroque of his youth. The Palladians, in the usual rejection by a new generation of the work of the preceding

one, detested the Chapel, but to us the minute distinctions between what they considered to be 'correct' and 'incorrect' are absurd. We can recognise what they could not, that Strahan's is a building of very high quality. It does have defects, however, the most glaring of which is the minimal relationship between its front and sides. Fortunately that doesn't matter much because few people have occasion to see the church in the round. The front is glorious, with a pediment supported by two pairs of Ionic pilasters, one on each side of a distinctly Wren-ish doorway. Above is a shell-headed niche, above that a baroque-ish semi-circular window. Its most memorable feature is the cupola, a wonderful, chunky, highly plastic invention, crowned with a deeply gadrooned lead dome like the stopper on a decanter. In 1740 it is inconceivable that Strahan had not seen several Palladian buildings, or at least a few of the by then numerous books of Palladian designs and philosophy. He ignored them, infuriated John Wood, and gave us one of Bristol's treasures. Not only us: a church 25 miles away in Somerset at Babbington shows its unmistakable influence.

The interior is no disappointment. Entry is through an octagonal lobby which supports the octagonal cupola above, and there is a baptistery and a vestry on either side of it. Over all three is a gallery. These are separated from the body of the chapel by a wall pierced by six arches, one in each of the three little rooms, and three in the gallery above. The wall is therefore a screen allowing views through the arches into the spaces beyond, creating a pleasing spatial complexity. Niches in the gallery and brackets in the entrance lobby support four busts by Rysbrack, the creator of William III triumphant on his horse in Queen Square.

As the exterior is glorified by the cupola, the interior is glorified by Thomas Paty's woodcarving, which covers the walls of the tiny chancel. The flowing trails of fruit, cherubs, flowers and wheat, etc. are cut with miraculous undercarving from pale limewood, which contrasts enchantingly with their dark oak background. In 1996 a thief caused appalling damage to the woodcarving by ripping away some saleable items such as doves and cherub heads. That, and a considerable amount of other damage which had occurred during the two and a half centuries since 1743, has been faithfully restored under the direction of the architect Glyn Leaman. The woodcarving was done by Charles Oldham of Frome. His workmanship is in every way the equal of Paty's, and Paty's work here has always been considered a miracle. This, the finest of Bristol's eighteenth-century churches, now looks in better shape that it can have done for well over a century.

The Exchange ★★★★★ Corn Street

1741-3

The cathedral, St Mary Redcliffe and the Exchange are Bristol's three truly great buildings. The Exchange was designed by the elder John Wood of Bath and built between 1741-3. The 1740s were boom years in Bristol, then the largest city and busiest port in the country after London. It was at the zenith of its prosperity, its huge wealth flowing in from its world-wide trade, which, alas, included slaving, the most profitable trade of all.

Wood's reputation was already nation-wide because of his ongoing transformation of Bath. In addition he was known in Bristol as a clever and resourceful engi-neer, having been prominent in the works to make the Avon navigable up to Bath and for having, nine years before, saved old St Nicholas's from collapse when John Padmore, the leading engineer in the west of England, had failed dismally to do so. By the time Wood was given the commission to design the Exchange he was beginning to become wealthy from his building speculations. Only 36, he was one hell of a fellow, and he knew it.

For years the city's merchants had traded in the limited shelter of the Tolzey's colonnade and in the street outside, using the four seventeenth-century bronze tables – the

famous Nails – which Wood moved as a historic relic to stand in front of his building. Outdoor trading was the norm in Europe; for example it was done at the Royal Exchange in London and at the Exchange in Amsterdam, so Wood's brief was to plan the Bristol Exchange's accommodation around an open court large enough to house 600 people. Ignoring this, he produced a plan with a roofed central area capable of holding that number. The highly conservative merchants, unaccustomed to the ways of architects, were appalled at such disobedience and ordered him to do as he was told. Not in the least chastened, he then designed a splendid court with a Corinthian colonnade instead of the arcades at the London and Amsterdam Exchanges. Time eventually proved him right. The nineteenth-century merchants refused to shiver in the rain any longer, and in 1870 had the court roofed to the design of E. M. Barry (son of the great Charles Barry who designed the Houses of Parliament). The present squalid glass roof, which hides Barry's fruity baroque work, was built in 1949.

All four of Wood's elevations survive in good condition, but the front is obviously the important one. He adapted the architectural system he had used 12 years earlier for the north side of Queen Square in Bath, but this time he had a much larger budget than he had been able to allow himself for his speculative houses there, so he was able to tighten up and enrich the design. The Exchange is only half the length of the Bath terrace – 11 bays instead of 23 – so he was able to omit the end pavilions, giving the Exchange crisper, tighter, proportions. Instead of Bath's six columns to support the pediment, the Exchange has four; its greater storey heights allowed him to raise its pilasters and columns on pedestals; and he could afford an expensive balustrade on the roof to add magnificence and tie everything together. Because this was one building and not seven, each requiring its own front door, the Exchange could have one magnificent central archway as an entrance. Finally, of course, this public building had to demonstrate Bristol's success and pomp, so it had to have, and the budget allowed it to have, much richer ornament than a row of private houses could be allowed. The pediment, conspicuously devoid of ornament in Bath, is filled with a magnificent achievement of the royal arms, and the spaces between the Corinthian capitals have heavily carved swags representing 'Great Britain and the Four Quarters of the World, with the chief Products and Manufactures of every Country'. The façade was recognised as one of the best of its type in the kingdom. The builder's son from Bath had stepped into the front rank.

As both of the identical side elevations face onto narrow lanes, Wood had to design them to be seen from close up, so he kept them plain. When you visit, look to see how cleverly he managed the tricky problem of composing a classical elevation which is partly three storeys and partly two. The rear elevation which faced onto an open market and contained some open-fronted market shops, could be seen easily, so it could be richer than the sides, though – quite properly – it is less magnificent than the ceremonial front. It is obscured by the glass roof built over the market in the nineteenth century and which disastrously hides two delightful little domes.

The cast-iron railings along the front are rare survivals from the mid-eighteenth century, as are the great nail-studded oak doors and knockers, all designed by Wood. The lovely vestibule is the only interior to survive in perfect condition. It should not be missed. The two minute hands on the clock are a reminder of pre-GMT days when Bristol time was behind London's.

The Exchange's ancillary buildings ★★★

Corn Street

1744, 1746, 1782

After construction of the Exchange was complete, the Corporation employed Samuel Glascodine, the Bristol carpenter who had been the demolition contractor on the site, to build the ancillary buildings, in 1744 the Market and in 1746 the Post Office. Of Glascodine's work on the market only the archway onto High Street survives. Based on the ancient triumphal arch motif it is pleasant enough but clumsy.

The Post Office, west of the Exchange on the other side of the narrow lane called, bizarrely, Exchange Avenue, is a much better design than the Market archway or anything else known to have been designed by Glascodine. I think Wood probably gave him a rough sketch. The narrow façade facing onto Corn Street (below) consists of three bays marked by long and short quoins, the central bay being projected slightly forward and capped by a tiny pediment. The ground floor consists of tall arches. All this produces a narrowly vertical composition which contrasts remarkably well with the horizontality of Wood's Exchange. The side elevation facing onto the lane is longer but based on the same compositional idea.

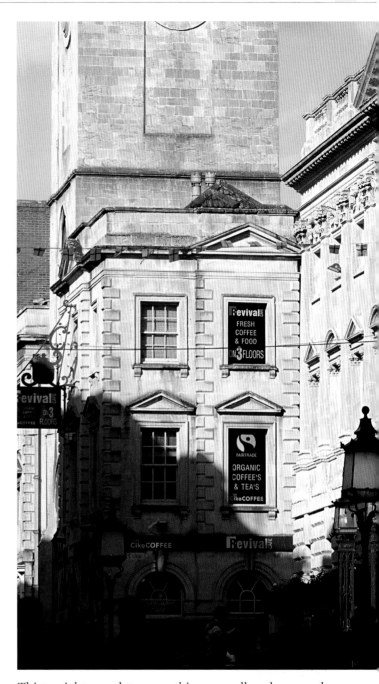

Thirty-eight years later something marvellous happened. In 1782 Thomas Paty was commissioned to build on the equivalent site east of the Exchange (above). With commendable modesty he repeated Glascodine's design, thus creating a symmetrical composition of which the Exchange is the centrepiece. This sort of opportunistic urban planning, though not unknown in the eighteenth century, was not common. It isn't common today, either.

Coopers' Hall ★★★   King Street

1743-4

Now the foyer of the Theatre Royal (q.v.)

When the Exchange was built, one of the buildings which had to be demolished to make way for it was the old and decrepit hall of the Coopers' Company. The Coopers agreed to sell it to the Corporation for £900 and a new site in King Street. The deal was negotiated for them by William Halfpenny, an ex-carpenter working as an architect and surveyor. The highly satisfied Coopers then gave him the commission to design their new hall (the only significant building known with certainty to have been designed by him, though he was probably responsible for others). He is best known now for his 19 pot-boiling architectural pattern books, and works on perspective and building geometry.*

The Hall he produced for the Coopers must have delighted them as much as it would have horrified sticklers for architectural restraint and purity such as John Wood of Bath. Halfpenny's façade, a piece of swaggering architectural braggadacio, appropriately fronted a hall much more noted for riotous dinners than decorous committee meetings. Today, in its new guise, it makes a marvellous theatre front, though perhaps slightly better suited to low comedy than high drama. Not the least of its attractions is its extraordinary contrast in scale with the adjoining almshouses. This sort of startling contrast is the very essence of picturesque street-making, and more than any other factor makes King Street such a pleasure for those with eyes to appreciate it.

* Until the end of the eighteenth century there were no architects in the modern sense of the word living in Bristol, that is, men who did nothing but design buildings and then supervised their construction by builders with whom they had no financial connection. As the entries in this book show, almost all the eighteenth-century buildings in Bristol were designed by craftsmen. The best carpenters and masons, though uneducated in anything but their trade, were highly intelligent men, as the best of their successors have to be today. Their grasp of the geometry necessary to cut highly complex three-dimensional non-orthogonal forms was, and still is, formidable. The designs in Halfpenny's architectural books are poor, but his books on constructional geometry have an impressive grasp of that mind-wrenching subject.

Clifton Hill House ★★★★   Clifton Hill

1746-50

Now a university hall of residence

Clifton Hill House was built between 1746-50 to the design of Isaac Ware, the universally respected architect, learned author, and Secretary of His Majesty's Board of Works, who, so it was said, was once a chimney-sweeper's boy with a passion for drawing who became the protégé of Lord Burlington, and was sent by him to study in Italy.

Clifton Hill House is the finest and most sophisticated of the houses built in the eighteenth century for the merchant families moving out of the congested and smoky city to enjoy the south-facing slopes of Clifton. Its site slopes steeply down from the road, so the street front is three storeys high and the garden front four. The lowest of these storeys, which makes up the fall in the ground and contained cellars at the back and service rooms on the garden side, is treated as a plinth extending on each side beyond the main block. The reception rooms were therefore a storey above garden level and were given a glorious double flight of steps down to it. This beautifully clear and logical system was severely compromised at some time in the nineteenth century when an additional storey was added to the wings.

Until Clifton Hill House was built, most windows of fashionable Bristol houses had projecting stone architraves (frames) around them, often with pediments on top. At Clifton Hill House the windows in the upper two storeys are simple holes cut in the ashlar walling with no decorative treatment whatever – no framing and no pediments. Below them the walling of the plinth is emphasised by deeply chan-

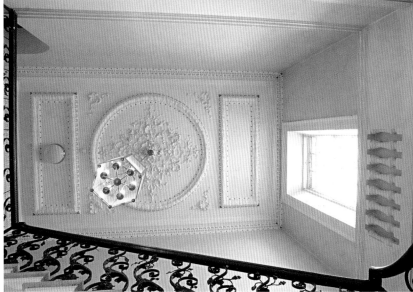

nelled ('rusticated') stonework. This was to have an enormous influence in Bristol, providing the basic pattern for many of the individual houses and terraces built at the end of the century and the early years of the next – rusticated stonework at ground level and plain ashlar with windows cut simply into it above.

Ware's writings make it clear that he would have much preferred his interior to have relatively simple Palladian plasterwork, but as he says regretfully in one of his books, the architect must pay regard 'to the fancy of the proprietor if he demanded French ornament' (by which he meant what we call rococo ornament), but should 'establish in his own mind the great superiority there is in the true and noble [Palladian] ornaments over these petty wildnesses. If he doesn't learn to do both he will do little in an age like this'. So he learnt those petty wildnesses and Clifton Hill House's plasterwork is delightfully rococo. It's hard to believe that in his heart of hearts, when he wasn't writing to educate architects and patrons, he didn't get some private pleasure from it.

Wesley's New Room ★★★★★ Broadmead

1739, 1748

Wesley and Whitefield's preaching to enormous outdoor crowds rather than always in churches, resulted in their being excluded from Established pulpits, so Wesley decided to build a chapel which would be free from interference by hidebound church dignitaries. In 1739 he bought this cheap plot just off Broadmead. It was surrounded on all sides by houses and reached only through a narrow lane off Horsefair. Here he built the world's first Methodist chapel. Not much is known about it because nine years later it was greatly enlarged by being extended towards Broadmead and given a narrow additional access from it. This is the building which survives today, extending from Broadmead to Horsefair. The name of its designer is unknown, but because of stylistic similarities with the nearby Friends' Meeting House in Quakers' Friars (now the Brasserie Blanc) which was designed by the highly gifted Bristol carpenter George Tully, it was probably designed and built (at a furious pace) by him.

He had to solve an appallingly difficult problem. The congregation was large and the site very small. It now extends full width from Broadmead to Horsefair because years later the Methodists bought and demolished the houses on both these streets which originally enclosed the site. The chapel therefore had to have galleries to cram everybody in. There was nothing unusual about that. The adjoining properties at the sides (some now demolished) severely limited the number and position of windows, so adequate daylight and ventilation could only be obtained by putting a large lantern in the roof. There was nothing unusual about that either. The difficulty was that a house for the resident minister and a large common room were required, but the chapel occupied every inch of ground. Tully solved this conundrum by building the residence and the common room on top of the chapel, and ran a large octagonal lightwell through the common room up to the lantern in the roof. He lit

the common room through windows in the sides of the octagon, which had the additional advantage of allowing the chapel to be supervised from above. The galleries and the living accommodation over them are supported by stone columns.

In place of the altar and reredos which provide the focus and climax of Anglican and Catholic churches, the chapel has a two-tier pulpit reached by a pair of stairs on either side leading down symmetrically from the side galleries. There is no ornament in the building and, apart from the unnecessary doubling of the stairs, nothing designed for show. The interior (there was no exterior) makes its point by its simple functionalism. Its powerful character comes from the urgent need to keep down costs; from the building's resultant simplicity; and from the ingenuity with which the problems were overcome. One does not have to be a Methodist, or even a Christian, to be moved by this enchanting, simple, building.

Goldney House and garden ★★★★
Clifton Hill
1720-64 Now a university hall of residence

The house was built for Thomas Goldney in about 1720, but was much altered and spoilt in 1865-8 when it was bought by Lewis Fry, the Quaker chocolate magnate. However, the garden front and one fine panelled room survive nearly intact. Goldney also was a Quaker, but with wonderfully elastic religious scruples. Much of his money came from gambling (forbidden to Quakers) in part ownership of two privateers (licensed pirates, forbidden). One of them struck gold – literally, and in enormous quantities – when it bloodily captured the Spanish treasure galleon off California (forbidden), sacked the city of Guayaquil (forbidden) and was then immortalised when it rescued Alexander Selkirk, the original of Robinson Crusoe.

The glory of the house is its garden. Most of it was created by Goldney's son, also Thomas and also an

equally Romantic home when the four-storey tower was built to house it in 1764.

While all this was going on, in 1753-4 Goldney laid out the great terrace, and sloping downhill from it, a curved bulwark pierced with circular 'gun ports'. At the top he built an enchanting Gothick rotunda from which to enjoy the panoramic view over the river to the country beyond. It originally had a circular colonnade around it. That has now gone but the battlements and the arched windows with their delightful glazing patterns survive. Four years later Goldney built the canal outside the house and installed the statue of Hercules. When I climbed illicitly into the garden at some date in the 1950s, there were sheep grazing on the long grass.

Garden visitors are often alleged to sigh 'Peace, perfect Peace'. Few visitors to Goldney's garden today are aware of how this particular island of peace was paid for. Time, as always, has obliterated the suffering which earned it and only the beauty remains.

elasticated Quaker. (His contribution to the achievement of peace on earth was the manufacture of cannons.) First, either he or his father built the orangery in c.1730 (re-faced in the 1930s). The famous grotto was started in 1737 and was structurally complete two years later.

For the next 25 years the family collected decorative local stones, including many Bristol diamonds (rock crystal from the Avon Gorge), fossils, shells and corals with which they encrusted every surface. They installed carvings of lions in their den, and Neptune in his cave holding a vase from which water tumbles towards the spectator. Imagine the effect when all this was illuminated in the darkness by the dim and flickering light of a flaming torch or a lantern. Even today, after being vandalised and in staid and unwavering electric light, the reflections of the plunging water make the sparkling surfaces of the walls and vaults coalesce into constantly changing shapes and creatures as you move around. In England only the grotto at Stourhead is better, and that is inferior to Goldney's in the treatment of its surfaces. His family's achievement in selecting and placing materials and directing craftsmen was unsurpassed. The engine which pumped the water was given its almost

Royal Fort House ★★★★ Tyndall's Avenue

1758-6 Now a department of the university

The house got its name from the large Royalist earthwork on the estate put up during the Civil War. In 1737 the merchant Thomas Tyndall leased the land and the existing house from the Corporation. Twenty one years later he built Royal Fort House, and bought the estate which he then had landscaped by the great Thomas Repton. At that time the land extended from St Michael's Hill, down to what are now Queen's and Whiteladies Roads, and up to the Downs.

In the nineteenth century all but a tiny remnant of the land was sold off as building lots (Cotham Hill, Hampton Road, Tyndall's Park Road etc), but the mansion survives, the best preserved of the large eighteenth-century houses in Bristol. Not much is known about the man who designed it, James Bridges. He arrived in the city in 1757 from America, and somehow picked up commissions for building Tyndall's house and rebuilding St Werburgh's and St Nicholas's churches. During this flurry of work, which must have increasingly upset the craftsmen in Bristol whose architectural role he was usurping, he was commissioned to design a replacement

for the ancient Bristol Bridge. Some of his rivals ganged up on him and managed to get his design rejected. Furious and hurt, in 1763, less than six years after having arrived, he left Bristol for the West Indies and disappeared from history. He was too hasty. In 1763 the Bridge Trustees changed their minds and appointed Thomas Paty to build the bridge to Bridges's design.

The external design of Royal Fort House is unusual; a severe cubic block without a portico or the wings which, in most houses of that date, would have tied it into the landscape. It is adjoined at the back by the old house, which Tyndall converted into the service quarters. The other three faces are all based on the same compositional idea: a flat wall which at the centre projects forward a few inches. This simple idea is varied on each front. The south has a tall bay window allowing Tyndall to make the most of what were then magnificent views down to Bristol and the river. It is, however, the poorest of the three façades, the windows on either side of the bay seeming to float aimlessly. The more successful north front contains the entrance, which is a remarkably modest

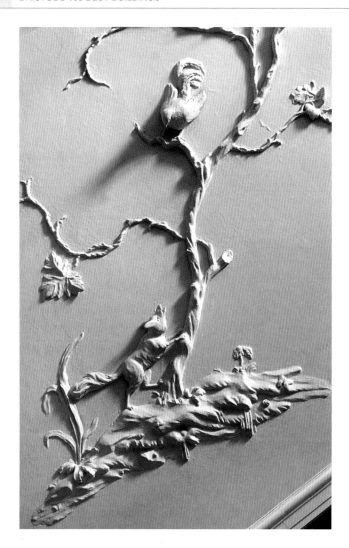

doorway, suggesting that Tyndall had no grandiose vision of himself. The west façade is beyond praise, the one which triumphantly justifies Bridges's decision not to give the house wings but to keep it as a simple block. The balance between plain ashlar and rusticated stonework, and the placing of the windows is masterly. Finally the parapet: it is worth spending a few minutes when you visit to study the clever way Bridges played games with it, making it alternately solid and balustraded, to emphasise the arrangement of the walls below.

If the exterior is relatively plain, the interior is spectacular, with wonderful woodcarving and plasterwork. The entrance hall is sternly Doric, divided by an arched screen from a Doric passage leading to the stair hall. In fact the entrance hall is not as stern as Bridges probably wanted, because the mood is contradicted by the playful rococo plasterwork on the walls. This ambiguous character is not continued into the stair hall, which is entirely rococo, with vines wantoning over the walls without the slightest respect for their individuality. One can admire

the craftsmanship without much liking the general effect. Opening off the entrance hall is the enchanting bay-windowed dining room, with Thomas Paty's rococo woodcarving and Thomas Stocking's plasterwork.

Bridges's academic (i.e. non-rococo) leanings are demonstrated by the room proportions which follow the ratios recommended by Palladio. The entrance hall is square, 1:1, with a screen dividing off a further space which, together with the hall, gives a ratio of 2:3. The drawing and dining rooms have the same ratio of 2:3, the study is square, and so on. These simple numerical ratios are common in Georgian buildings and probably always indicate their architect's underlying classical, Palladian, instincts. (See the entry on Clifton Hill House to read what one such architect felt about the fashion for rococo ornament.)

Kings Weston stables and ice house ★★★

Napier Miles Road, Kings Weston. Ice house not open

1763

While Robert Southwell the third, squire of Kings Weston, was in Rome on his Grand Tour, he met the young Robert Mylne who was building an enviable reputation there as a student of architecture. Mylne came from a highly distinguished line of Scottish mason-architects and engineers. On his return to Britain in 1761 he immediately confirmed his brilliance by winning the competition for Blackfriars Bridge in London at the age of 27. Two years later Southwell invited him to Bristol to design new stables a few hundred yards from the house.

The stables are on the north side of the road and originally formed two open-sided quadrangles, the wings of the northern of which have been demolished. Fortunately this has not damaged an extremely clever piece of planning. The three sides of the southern quadrangle face onto the road. The wings terminate in pedimented gable ends which are faced on the opposite side of the narrow road by the identically pedimented gables of two small pavilions. Between them is a pool which exactly mirrors the stable court, and behind it a garden and high wall which echo the middle range of the stables, thus completing the quadrangle in a symmetrical composition bisected by the road. This symmetry is not immediately appreciated by the viewer but is enormously satisfying when it becomes apparent. Nowadays rarely seen except by locals, it is one of the most successful pieces of classical planning in Bristol.

The pool was as much an aesthetic pleasure then as it is now, but it was also severely practical. It was probably an occasional swimming pool, and it provided water for the horses, fish for the table and ice for the ice house which survives in a clump of trees a hundred or so metres to the north-west. Ice houses came in several forms of which the best and most expensive was the type built here. It is a large inverted brick cone sunk four or so metres into the ground, with its domed top covered in insulating earth, bushes and trees. The sloping entrance passage was fitted with a series of three or four doors, some spaced far enough apart to accommodate one or two small pantries. In winter (usually much colder then than now) men collected all the ice from the pool, smashed it into powder and shovelled it into the cone. Labourers stationed inside then rammed it down, sprinkling it with water as they did so, causing it to set into a solid mass. Throughout the year the doors were kept firmly closed and the spaces between them insulated with great straw mattresses. When in summer the ice began to melt, it slid down the cone's sides whilst remaining in a solid lump. A sump at the bottom was fitted with a pump so that melted water could be discharged. Perishables could be stored in the pantries as in a fridge today. The availability of ice throughout the year made it possible to chill foods and drinks.

Theatre Royal ★★★★   King Street

1763-6

Before electricity, theatres were lit by a multitude of candles. The scenery, painted on canvas stretched on wooden frames, was highly inflammable. The consequences were predictable, so very few survive. Bristol's Theatre Royal is the oldest in Britain to be still in use.

Thomas Paty was commissioned to build the theatre in 1763, given drawings prepared by the staff carpenter of Drury Lane Theatre, and told to follow them 'as nearly as the circumstances of the ground will permit'. Since his site was part of the small back garden of a house in Baldwin Street, with no street frontage, and only accessible through a lane between houses in King Street, they can't have been much help. The plan he produced was a horseshoe instead of the then Drury Lane's rectangular auditorium, and had two tiers but no gallery. The theatre was completed in 1766 to general satisfaction, which despite some sore bums from the few remaining hard benches in the gallery and cricked necks from inconvenient columns, it gives to this day.

In 1800 a gallery was squeezed in by sloping up the previously flat ceiling. It seems likely that most of the present lower two tiers and probably re-used bits of the sloping ceiling are Paty's work. The colours also are probably more or less those chosen by him, since it is known that the original colour scheme was green and gold. The stage projected a couple of metres further forward into the house than at present, so the end boxes were behind the front of the stage and faced directly onto it. This extraordinary arrangement was usual at that time.

In 1903 the purchase of a house allowed a peculiarly depressing frontage onto King Street to be built. It survived until 1970, when Peter Moro, one of the architects of London's Festival Hall, gave the theatre new backstage facilities and converted the Coopers' Hall (q.v.) into the foyer. The price of progress was the loss of most of the ancient stage machinery. Fortunately it was possible to preserve the thunder run because it was out of the way in the roof. It consists of a zig-zag series of wooden troughs down which cannon balls were rolled. Those who have seen it operated say that it was terrifying as the cannon balls leapt and bounced down, making a convincing sound of thunder over the heads of the audience. Fear that one day a cannon ball, like a thunder bolt from Jove, would crash through the ceiling in the ultimate *coup de théâtre*, has persuaded modern managements not to use it. The cannon balls are now locked away.

Albemarle Row ★★ Hotwells

1763

This terrace of eight houses, designed by Thomas Paty, was built in 1763 for a speculator called John Webb as lodgings for visitors to the nearby Hot Well, then at the peak of its success. Webb's initials and the date are carved in a stone cartouche in the pediment of the central house.

The façades are of red brick with stone dressings and door surrounds, a fashion that had lasted since the first houses were built in Queen Square just after 1700 and was to end its reign with the rise of stucco towards the end of the century. As one would expect with anything designed by Thomas Paty, the individual house fronts are excellent, especially the beautiful central house with its pediment. But that raises a question. The classic statement of a terrace of houses grouped symmetrically on either side of a central pedimented house was John Wood's north side of Queen Square in Bath, and it was he who had explained its rationale 'to group ordinary town houses in such a way as to gain the effect of a single palace'. Now nobody looking at Albemarle Row would think for a moment that it's a single palace because the slope of the ground means that each house has to step down from its neighbour, declaring unmistakably its individuality. So why stress the central house in this way? John Wood himself and subsequent architects in hilly Bath recognised the slight absurdity of doing this, and set the English pattern for such sites: don't stress any of the houses, recognise that large central pediments are best reserved for flat sites and are inappropriate for sloping ones.

Some of the houses have delightful, but appallingly neglected and decaying, decorative ironwork panels in their railings, and lampholders over their doors. The small end house, obviously a later addition, has an interesting detail worth looking at. In eighteenth-century England the most admired brickwork was the most regular and consistent. Unfortunately hand-made bricks, then all that were available, warp and bow in the kiln and vary greatly in length. The only way the bricklayer could accommodate them in perfect courses, with the vertical joints kept in line up the height of the wall, was either to select only even-sized bricks or to have wide joints. We admire the rough tweedy texture which wide joints produce but the Georgians hated it. They wanted fine joints, and some clever fellow invented a way of achieving them cheaply – or rather, of appearing to achieve them. It was called tuck pointing and was used on the end house of Albemarle Row. The mortar was coloured to match the colour of the brickwork by mixing brick dust into it, and the joints were made flush. In consequence they didn't show up much. The disguised joint was then lightly scored and a very thin line of almost liquid lime mortar was drawn onto it to make an apparent joint. The effect is surprisingly convincing, but it is curious to see how often the artificial and real joints diverge. Unless one looks very closely, the effect is of exquisitely fine brickwork. Unfortunately the lime washes off after a few centuries and tuck pointing is now fading away and becoming rare. On the end house it is best seen in the protected area under the bay window, particularly on the right-hand side where the brick-coloured mortar can be seen clearly, and the vertical tuck pointed joints are well to the side of some real joints. (The best example I know is on the façade of Lunsford House, high above the north side of Park Row.)

Arnos Court, Black Castle and gateway ★★★

Bath Road, Brislington

1760, 1764 House, now a hotel and the Castle pub

The house was built in about 1760 by William Reeve, a wealthy copper smelter and brass founder. It is fairly routine Georgian Gothick, where each classical detail has been replaced by a routine Gothick equivalent. This play-acting Gothic is an English sub-branch of the international rococo. Inside the house the stairway and one room contain excellent examples of the more usual rococo plasterwork of curlicues, foliage and fantastic birds.

Bristol's copper smelting industry produced a hard, slightly iridescent black slag which was cast into the triangular-shaped copings still to be seen on walls in the older parts of Bristol. Reeve went further. Like other landowners of his time he had antiquarian tastes and indulged them by building his stables, brewhouse and laundry in the form of a fake castle sited downwind from his house on the other side of the Bath Road which crossed his land. That wasn't very original but his building material certainly was. He used his black slag cast into large blocks, arousing universal comment from the fascinated travellers who passed every day. People of sensibility were expected to shudder at castles and dungeons, monks and ruins. Sham castles were becoming commonplace, but a black one …

The castle was built in 1764 by the Patys, who probably designed it, taking most of the details from the Gothick pattern books of the time. It is built around a courtyard with turrets at the corners, a tower over the entrance and another tower facing it on the opposite side of the court. They have the usual battlements, arrow slits, traceried windows and buttresses. Hidden high on the top floor of the back tower there is a tiny room with delicate plasterwork, the only elegant room in the building. Innocent historians have always said it was the chapel. It clearly wasn't: it has no religious imagery and room only for a dining table, a couple of chairs and a chaise-longue. Quaker Reeve liked to do some of his entertaining well away from home.

Originally the stables were entered through an archway into a forecourt. The forecourt was destroyed in 1911 to make way for a new road, and the archway moved to its present position facing up the Bath Road. It was built with niches to take four medieval statues which Reeve bought in 1769 and 1771 from two of Bristol's ancient city gates, which were being demolished at that time. There are also two niches left vacant to receive figures which would turn up later. They never did because

Reeve became bankrupt in 1774, just before his arch was finished. The uncut blocks over the arch were intended to be carved with a coat of arms, presumably his (though such signs of earthly pride were forbidden to Quakers) and other blocks were going to become the capitals and bases of the columns. Today nobody would be deceived into thinking that this is a genuine medieval arch, but only 20 years after it was finished, the draughtsman S. H. Grimm, and apparently everybody else, believed it to be one of Bristol's medieval gateways which Reeve had moved here. It was this which saved it in 1911 when it was about to be demolished. There was such an outcry that it was moved to its present position.

In 1898 the medieval figures were removed to the Museum. In 1994, when I restored the archway on behalf of the Bristol Development Corporation, the Museum declined to put them back so I commissioned Sue Dring to carve the excellent replicas.

Christ Church, City **★★★★**   Corn Street
1786, 1883

The church, a replacement of an ancient medieval building, was designed in 1786 by William Paty, the first academically trained architect to live and work in Bristol. He was 28 when he got the job, having, no doubt, received the craftsman's training of all the members of his brilliant family, in addition to his architectural education at the Royal Academy.

At that time English architects particularly admired St Martin-in-the-Fields in London, so it's not surprising that young Paty took it as the basis of his design, with influences from one or two more recent buildings as well. Nonetheless, he had digested these influences and produced something original and marvellous. His nave is separated from each aisle by three tall columns sitting on high pedestals to lift their bases above the high box pews which at that time filled the church. Since they were replaced by much lower Victorian bench pews, the columns now look more lanky than Paty would have liked. Unlike St Martin's, Christ Church has no side

galleries, so the two aisles and the nave form a single large airy space. The roof consists of shallow rectangular saucer domes, those over the nave aligned north-south, those over the aisles east-west.

By 1883 fashion had made its inevitable revolution and Paty's work was considered ugly and utterly unsuitable for a place of worship, so the congregation asked the architect Henry Williams to bring it as up to date as possible, and to get rid of what were then called 'heathen Grecian furnishings'. So out went Paty's box pews, windows, reredos, altar, communion rails and tiny mahogany baluster font, and in came new windows (which must, even in the 1880s, have been considered uninspired), and a reredos which is appallingly intrusive in Paty's interior.

By the 1920s the wheel of fashion had turned again and late-eighteenth century buildings and furnishings were coming back into popular esteem. So back came the altar, rails and font, which some sentimentalist had put into the vaults instead of the fire, and back from the vaults came the surviving bits of the reredos which were then pieced together and re-erected as a chancel screen. Unfortunately Williams's heavy-handed reredos and windows survive to detract from this lovely interior.

On the street front Williams restricted himself to replacing the entrance with a rather attractive Italian renaissance design. It is discordant in this location but fortunately a minor discord because the far more important tower and spire above it survive intact. They are a simplified version of the steeple at St Martin-in-the-Fields, and although inferior to that superlative work, are clever and hugely enjoyable, making a vital contribution to the central city's skyline.

Paty must have particularly enjoyed replacing the quarter-jacks – the two colourful figures over the entrance which strike the quarter hours – which his grandfather had carved for the earlier church. William Paty died in 1800 at the age of 42, a severe loss to architecture in the city.

Hope Chapel ★   Hope Chapel Hill, Hotwells
1788

Towards and just after the end of the eighteenth century it became the fashion for unemployed aristocratic ladies to found establishments for worthy causes, such as Lady Isabella King's Home for Distressed Gentlewomen at Bailbrook House in Bath, or the Countess of Huntingdon's many chapels. Hope Chapel was founded by the Ladies Hope and Glenorchy to stem the tide of

pews treated them as property to be bought and sold, rented or bequeathed. A family pew in a respectable area sold for £100 to £150. In 1863 one owner had 13 in St Andrew's, the Clifton parish church.)

Hope Chapel's façade is basically classical in its composition, but dressed in the more Christian-seeming Gothic. Beside the Gothic windows are two pilasters

wickedness they saw engulfing Clifton. After their deaths the Chapel was opened in 1788 by another pious patroness, Lady Maxwell. The noble ladies were clearly not bothered by lower-class sin as all the pews were for rent. This effectively excluded Clifton's huge servant and trade population, though a few pews at the back were presumably rented for the footmen who accompanied their employers to their highly select and fashionable Divine Service. (In all Anglican churches the owners of

supporting a cornice above which the parapet rises into a sort of pediment containing the words 'Hope Chapel'. The whole façade is rendered and scribed in imitation of masonry. It is utterly ridiculous and yet utterly delightful. The name of the designer is unknown.

St Paul's ★★★★ Portland Square

1789-94 Now a circus school

In the 1780s the new population of the recently completed streets around Brunswick Square had caused overcrowding at the local parish church of St James, and the imminent completion of the Square and the start of Portland Square and its associated streets would obvi-

ously make the situation untenable. As described in the previous entry, in that period prosperous people bought pews, and either used them themselves or rented them out as an investment, thus driving out the poor who so dreadfully lowered the tone. By the late 1780s even

rented pews were unobtainable at St James's. As their availability, like parking spaces today, affected house prices and rents, Daniel Hague, the builder architect who was developing Portland Square, had a powerful interest in seeing that a new church was built. As a result of his pushing, in 1789 the Corporation obtained an Act of Parliament which carved the new parish of St Paul out of St James's, and after the usual bit of eighteenth-century chicanery, Hague was commissioned to design it.

Work began immediately and was completed in 1794. Hague's design is Gothic, but the pointed arches are purely cosmetic. Everything, even the tower, is essentially classical in feeling, making it a perfect foil to the much more severe neo-classical houses in the Square. St Paul's is a perfect example of the pendulum of fashion. When it was new it was an 'elegant structure'; a century later, in 1893, Latimer called it ugly; in 1923 it reached its nadir when Dening called it a monstrosity. 29 years later, Ison almost liked it, but considered the interior to be more suited to an assembly room than a church. In 1965 I called it 'a magnificent airy space, quite breathtaking after one enters through the vestibule', but I was much less enthusiastic about the tower. Now, 45 years later, I consider it the best in the city after St Mary Redcliffe. The pendulum has completed its swing.

By great good fortune the tower is still a prominent feature in many views of Bristol. It was rumoured when it was built that it was designed by the new vicar, and it is indeed quite likely that he did produce an amateur sketch, because its design of repeated set-backs is not a logical stone structure, though it would be much more so if it were built of timber. Despite that theoretical objection, the tower is a stunning ornament to the square and to the city.

Sion Hill **** Clifton
c1780-90

Towards the end of the eighteenth century all of Clifton's south facing grandstand sites were in the hands of builders, but because people were still wanting to move into the area, the land at the top became interesting to speculators. Moreover, Hotwells and the lower slopes of Clifton were becoming less fashionable. At the height of the Hot Well's popularity it attracted people of all ages, usually more interested in its social life than its cure for 'hot livers, feeble brains and red pimply faces'. By the end of the eighteenth century it was attracting the seriously ill, and the adjacent Dowry Parade became known as Death Row, not an attraction for prospective permanent residents.

It is curious that the land facing west along the gorge's brow had not been snapped up earlier to take advantage of its stunning views. After about 1780 this began to happen, largely through the efforts of a developer called Thomas Morgan who had started his career as a lawyer. He had an idea that still seems extraordinarily bold, that if he were to drill a deep borehole on the top of the cliff immediately above the Hot Well, he would tap into it. Without any of the huge apparatus of geological testing and background knowledge available today, he did so with triumphant success. Having drilled nearly 250 feet to a level well below the river bed his pipe produced 34,000 gallons a day. He named it the Sion Spring and built a Pump Room on the site of the old St Vincent Rocks Hotel (now flats) to house it. (When some years later the hotel was built, the pipe was extended across the road to what is now the ballroom of the Avon Gorge Hotel.) In addition to servicing his spa he used the water to supply 300 houses, most of which he developed himself.

Amongst Morgan's many housing speculations are the Mall and Sion Hill. They make a fascinating contrast: East and West Malls consist of more-or-less identical houses; Sion Hill is a wonderful mixture. Some houses are wide, some narrow; some are three-storeyed, some are four. Some have flat fronts and others, in order to gain the widest possible views, have bow fronts or canted bays. In building construction the more repetition there is, the less the unit cost will be. Sion Hill's site justified higher building costs because they looked out to the Somerset countryside, whilst those in the Mall looked at each other. Sion Hill was built in the 1780s and '90s.

Later, early in the next century, further variety was added when owners added balconies, or if they already had them, added metal canopies over them. At that time fashion, much influenced by what was happening in Brighton and the other south-coast resorts, favoured the painting of these tent-like canopies in black and white, or green and white vertical stripes. They add enormously to the vitality of the scene.

Time has been kind to Sion Hill. Because of its unique situation it never suffered to the same degree the social decline of Georgian Clifton, and the houses, at least on their street fronts, have not suffered from much subsequent alteration. It is hard to think of any other residential street in Bristol which is so sparklingly attractive.

Windsor Terrace ★★ Clifton
1790-1811

As architecture Windsor Terrace is a disaster; as scenery it is superlative; as a building speculation, a ghastly warning.

In the late 1780s and early 1790s Bristol went through a bout of house-building mania. All anyone needed was an idea and a banker, and bankers, as we have rediscovered, are as eager when they scent a profit as a whore in a gold rush.

In April 1791 a Bristol newspaper reported that 'ground is actually taken for more than 2000 houses'. That figure is put into context if we realise that on a very rough computation there were only about 12,000 houses in the city at that time, and there was not the slightest reason to expect a sudden surge in the population. People had gone mad. The mania collapsed in the spring of 1793, when all building came to a sudden stop. Within a few months there were over 50 bankruptcies, including several banks whose fall produced yet more failures. Over 500 houses in Bristol, a large proportion of them in Clifton, were left unfinished. Some were just holes in the ground, some almost complete. It was to be more than 30 years before they were all finished.

The most insane speculation of all, and surely the most hopeless building ever started anywhere, was Windsor Terrace. It was begun at the peak of the mania in 1790 on a precipice in the Avon Gorge. Two houses at its eastern end are built on roughly level ground, but before the other eight could be started an enormous platform had to be built out into the gorge to support them. It had to be broad enough to take the houses, the pavement, the road and, for some bizarre reason, a strip

of grass as well. On its southern side and western end the platform is a stupendous man-made cliff jutting out into the gorge. It was colossally expensive. The man who had it built was William Watts, who had made a fortune by inventing a better way to manufacture lead shot. He did it by pouring the molten metal through a sieve into a tank of water at the bottom of a tower. Having realised the alchemists' dream of transmuting lead into gold, he poured it into the bottomless tank of his Windsor Terrace platform. Being richer than the other speculators he lasted a few months longer than them, but finally crashed without having completed a single house.

The ten he had started were eventually completed as cheaply as possible by a builder who made no attempt to complete the classical dressing which had been planned by Watts's architect, John Eveleigh of Bath. The result is an appalling mess. Not one house can be looked at without a shudder. But the terrace and its man-made cliff is one of the great and visually indispensable buttresses of Clifton in the famous views from the south and west. Posterity owes a lot to William Watts.

Royal York and Cornwallis Crescents ★★

Clifton

1791-1818, 1792-1825

In the mid-eighteenth century Clifton's slope, like the Avon Gorge of which it was the south-facing extension of its eastern side, was almost entirely covered by trees and the occasional exposed rockface. Hotwells had become built-up at the bottom, and there were some

contour. Both were designed by William Paty, and neither is much shakes as architecture. The Patys were in danger of becoming something of a bore at this time because, wherever they built houses, and they built hundreds and hundreds, they gave them identical windows with five overlapping voussoirs, profitably mass-produced in their masons' yard.

The two crescents make an interesting contrast. Royal York is stuccoed on both faces, Cornwallis only on its

mansions and cottages at the top. With only a few exceptions nobody dared to face the difficulties, both constructional and financial, of building on the slope, which at the western end approaching the gorge was increasingly vertiginous. However, the great increase in middle-class affluence meant that there was a pool of people who would leap at the opportunity of joining the rich to enjoy the sunshine and the grandstand views.

The most desirable sites were on the higher slopes, so these were the first to go. Royal York Crescent (above), started in 1791, is built along a contour that twists along and just below the brow. Cornwallis Crescent, started in the following year, follows its own, not quite parallel,

north side, but faced with Bath stone on its south. Another difference is the greater length of Royal York, said to be the longest terrace in Britain, but the really profound difference is that Royal York is built on the north and Cornwallis on the south of their access roads. When terraces are aligned east-west, as these are, the north sides are inevitably rather gloomy – they don't have the balconies which so enliven the south sides, and because they front the less important rooms, are sometimes festooned with pipes from the kitchens and bathrooms which were inserted in the twentieth century. So Royal York Crescent turns its cheerful face to the road, to be enjoyed by everybody, and its back to its overshadowed and relatively unattractive gardens. Cornwallis (below) is the opposite. Passers-by have to endure its long and tedious back, but the garden front, its honey-coloured Bath stone glowing even on dull days, is enjoyed only by its residents.

Royal York Crescent's great length forms most of the skyline in the view of Clifton from the south. Its roof could be as boring as the interminable rows of windows, but it has evolved in a fascinating and picturesque way. After about 1840 this southern part of Clifton declined

picturesque tattiness. If these changes had been inflicted on a building of real architectural merit it would have been a tragedy, but here it has been an improvement.

Long before either Crescent was complete the great crash of 1793 occurred. Building everywhere stopped abruptly. The half-built shells remained for decades. Throughout Bristol the streets of increasingly tottering walls looked to visitors like a city destroyed by bombardment. Royal York Crescent was finally completed in

socially when Georgian architecture went out of fashion, and as always happens to big houses when that occurs, most of them were subdivided into rooms and flats. To increase their rents, landlords built extensions on their roofs, and then further extensions, huts and lean-tos onto them. Tidy-minded planners hate them and refuse to allow any more, but people who judge with their eyes and not from mental rule books love the way they have enlivened an otherwise uninteresting skyline. A rather similar thing has happened to the balconies, which William Paty undoubtedly wanted to be uniform with only minor variations of ironwork. Over years they have been patched, replaced and altered into their present

1818, Cornwallis not until 1825, thirty-three years after it was started.

Both crescents have wide terraces on their south sides built over vaults, which at Royal York, since they face onto the road, have turned out to be useful as garages. Although both terraces were private, that at Royal York, since it is easily accessible from the road, has become public: the most glorious promenade in Bristol. Cornwallis's terrace has remained private and faces onto its huge communal garden of great lawns and wooded slopes, a paradise for children, away from any roads and supervised by the terrace and 315 windows.

Clifton Assembly Rooms ★★★ The Mall

1806-11 Now the Clifton Club, shops etc

In the years around 1800 every British community had to have its assembly rooms. They had been around for a long time, but Beau Nash's remarkable achievement with the Rooms in Bath, which were known to every family in polite society, gave the idea a huge impetus. So as Clifton's population began to grow it was inevitable that it should want its own rooms. In 1806 a magnificent site became available looking down the gardens between West and East Malls, and attached to it a firm describing itself as 'stonemasons, architects, builders, etc' consisting of three Greenway brothers. The site was acquired and the Greenways told to design and build it. They did, but Francis, the architect brother, never saw it complete.

What happened was this. Whilst the firm was building the Rooms they were also completing the half-built shell of 34 Cornwallis Crescent on behalf of a client when they became bankrupt. Francis said they were owed £250 for additional work over and above the contract figure, but had lost the written instruction to do it. Their client said he had never issued it and had not authorised any extra work. After some delay Francis said he had found the instruction, signed by the client's solicitor. It was a forgery. He was tried at Bristol Assizes, pleaded guilty and was sentenced to death. It was the best thing that ever happened to him. After a horribly long period waiting to be hanged his sentence was commuted to life transportation to Botany Bay. There were no architects in Sydney and the Governor wanted one. Greenway must have been a personable fellow, the Governor took to him, and he built numerous government buildings, finally dying respected and admired, already recognized as The Father of Australian Architecture. In the 1950s he received the ultimate accolade of having his portrait engraved on one of Australia's banknotes: not bad for a forger.

The façade of the Assembly Rooms was, and still could be, a marvellously rich and plastic composition of nine separate elements. The boldly projecting centrepiece with its Ionic columns and grand pediment is flanked on either side by a narrow deeply recessed and shadowed bay, then by a wide projecting bay, then another shadowed recession, and finally, at each end, by a wide projecting bay with a curved front. There is no other street façade in Bristol showing such assured mastery of plastic composition. Unfortunately it was spoilt when Georgian architecture was out of fashion, first, in 1856 by the row of two-storey shopfronts which smother the right hand side, and then in 1894 by the heavy oriels jammed into two of Greenway's windows in the centrepiece.

Whilst Greenway was waiting for the hangman, the interior was completed by Joseph Kay. The ballroom is the best of his rooms, but impressive rather than beautiful. To some extent that is probably due to the dismal decoration and furnishing. It wouldn't be difficult to make a substantial improvement.

The Paragon ★★★ Clifton

1809-14

John Drew, the builder who completed poor bankrupt William Watts's half-built houses at Windsor Terrace (q.v.), presumably made some money by doing so. He wanted more. Somehow managing to blind himself as to why Watts had become bankrupt, in 1809 he leased the almost equally cliff-like land above, and set about building a crescent of 21 houses. As at Windsor Terrace this would only be possible by first constructing a great vaulted platform on which to sit the houses. He wasn't quite as foolhardy as Watts, because his crescent would at least follow the curve of the hillside and not run into the huge cost of contradicting it. Nonetheless he had caught the mania. All around him were the already decaying and tottering walls of abandoned half-built houses. No matter: he would succeed where they failed. Perhaps he nearly did because he completed 10 houses, but the money from them was not enough to cover the

sums he had spent. Like Watts and all the others, he fell.

Again following what had happened at Windsor Terrace, another builder took over the lease of the land, bought the uncompleted buildings, altered the design by adding a storey and, most of the risk having been taken by Drew, finished successfully. Finally, some years later, a much larger house was added at the western end of the Crescent to enjoy the unparalleled views.

The Paragon is not the paragon that Drew intended, but despite the change of design halfway along, and the entirely different end house, it is perhaps the best of Clifton's Georgian terraces, which, architecturally speaking, are a relatively poor lot. Drew's houses at the eastern end of the Crescent are the best, but of course the glory is that the whole Crescent forms the towering western prow of the great heap of piled-up terraces that makes the panorama of Clifton one of England's most famous views.

The Commercial Rooms ★★ Corn Street

1810   Now a bar

The Commercial Rooms were built in 1810 as coffee rooms for the merchants and lawyers working in the central city. It was the first major work of the 24-year-old Charles Busby, who had had a brilliant student career at the Royal Academy. Before he got the job, the secretary and chairman of the club had visited Liverpool and Manchester to look at buildings designed by Thomas Harrison. It seems that these clients gave young Mr Busby very precise instructions about how the club should be planned and look. It has been said that the building he gave them was the first to introduce the Greek Revival into Bristol. This is only partially true; the 'feel' of the front and the details of the interior are Greek, but the order of the Ionic columns in the portico is Roman (taken from the Theatre of Marcellus in Rome).

The exterior is a delightfully sensitive and delicate composition of receding planes. The four slender columns and pediment stand slightly forward from the narrow side wings, and provide the cover for an open porch. A metre or so behind the portico and wings rises the low wall fronting the Great Room behind it. The pediment and the side wings support stone figures of Commerce, Navigation and Bristol. To my eyes they are rather too big for this tiny façade but they give it what the members no doubt wanted – an impressively classical finish. (It is fascinating how these business men wanted their commercial activities to be held in trappings redolent of learning and tradition, as far as possible from money making.)

The interior consists of the ambitiously titled Great Room, which in fact is not very big, and a smaller reading room behind it. Since the surrounding buildings made windows impossible, both rooms are lit from above. The spectacular feature is the Great Room's dome supported on posts disguised as caryatids, its circle adapted to the square room by curved triangular planes known as pendentives. The wind dial is a reminder of the days when the direction of the wind, and therefore the time of arrival or departure of ships into or from the harbour, would have been urgent information for some of the merchants dining in the Rooms.

The Rooms are now occupied by a bar. The colour scheme looks as though it was designed by a demented paint salesman.

Blaise Hamlet ★★★★★ Hallen Road, Henbury

1810-11 Now administered by the National Trust

Blaise Hamlet was designed by John Nash, one of my great heroes, but not usually very popular with the critics, poor things, who have always thought him a bit flash.

The Hamlet was built in 1810-11 for John Scandrett Harford, the Bristol banker, who had not joined the Gadarene rush of the 1790s. He asked Nash to design ac-

Harford was a decent man and instead of sacking Nash for impudence took his words to heart and did as he suggested. He then told people about it and didn't try to take the credit for himself.

The Hamlet is a few hundred metres downhill from Harford's gates, hidden by trees from the road, and

commodation for his retired employees, and expected to get the usual row of almshouses. Harford later told the architect C. R. Cockerell that Nash then gave him a short but impassioned lecture. Cockerell was so impressed that he noted it in his diary:

> He recommended to Mr Harford to build his alms Houses in a picturesque manner & in a retired spot & not in a row. He says the pride which is natural to men & makes them ashamed of receiving alms is an honourable one & should not be crushed ... nor is it well to tarnish a benevolent motive with the blazon of a coat of arms & an inscription setting forth the liberality of the Founder.

approached obliquely by a narrow path through the trees so that one comes upon it unexpectedly. It consists of nine cottages, one of them double, scattered with complete informality around a slightly undulating green. Slightly off centre is the village pump (replaced and re-dated 1859). All the cottages are built of the local rubble stonework, but everything else is varied. Some walls are straight, some are curved. The roofs of thatch and stone slates curl and dip around them. The variety of their shapes and chimneys would fill a textbook. Nothing is regular, nothing repeated. Wherever you look, the variety of invention is enchanting and, for an architect, humbling.

Several writers have compared Harford's Hamlet with Marie Antoinette's Hameau at Versailles. Quite apart from the fact that Harford's housed retired workers and the Queen's housed bored ladies playing at it, there is no comparison. Blaise is an architectural jewel and the Hameau a pretentious stage set. Architecture never lies, no matter how much the architect tries to do so.

Whilst an assistant* was converting Nash's quick sketches and verbal instructions into drawings for the builder, Nash himself was working on his first ideas for Regent's Park. Its basic concept is identical to the Hamlet's: a Romantic scatter of variegated buildings around a green, but huge classical terraces instead of tiny picturesque cottages. Both are superb.

* The assistant was George Repton, son of the great Humphry. Because his notebooks containing drawings of the cottages survive and Nash's sketches and instructions don't, modern writers tend to attribute their design to both men, or even to Repton alone. This is absurd. Repton was Nash's tool, no more. There is nothing in his subsequent career to suggest anything more than modest talent, whilst Nash's career sparkled with genius.

The Old Council House ★★★ Corn Street

1824-7

Bristol has had four Council Houses so far, of which this is the third. It was designed by Robert Smirke, no doubt because of the success of his St George's church on Brandon Hill, which was the first in the city to be fully designed in the Greek Revival style. His Council House, also Grecian, was started in 1824 and completed in 1827 on the site of its eighteenth-century predecessor and the demolished St Ewen's church.

Whenever Sir Robert Smirke's buildings are discussed nowadays they tend to be belittled, I think unfairly. He was not an outstandingly imaginative designer and sometimes tended to repeat himself. The Council House's façade onto Corn Street, for example, is similar to the one he was designing at the same time for the Royal College of Physicians in Trafalgar Square. But even so, it is a fine, reticent and dignified front, entirely suitable for its symbolic purpose, and vastly better than its lumpen successor on College Green (q.v.). The relatively few remains of ancient Greek buildings to survive from antiquity were then supplying architects with plenty of decorative details, but nothing survived, if it had ever existed, which could guide them in designing a building of this type, unless their clients were prepared to surround it with a colonnade like the Parthenon. Smirke's design is basically a wide four-bay frontispiece projecting very slightly in front of narrow one-bay wings. A very heavy entablature runs across the façade, breaking forward with the frontispiece. The central two bays are recessed to emphasise the entrance. The cills of the first-floor windows and a heavy band of ornament below them, also run across the façade, but, unlike the entablature, stop at each of the six pilasters, looking as though they penetrate through them. I find this a very satisfying design, though somewhat pushed into the background by its much more exuberant Corn Street neighbours.

Just inside the entrance is the magnificent stair. Its balusters are Doric columns made of brass, and its treads are inlaid with brass fretwork. There is nothing unimaginative about that. The Council Chamber is the finest and richest – and least known – Regency interior in Bristol. It is lit by a circular lantern in the sumptuous ceiling. Lovers of architecture should try to see it.

In 1829 the small Magistrates' Court was built next door, with a façade made deliberately quiet so as not to compete with the Council House, and in 1898 a new and much bigger Council Chamber was built at the back. Lovers of architecture should try to avoid it.

Bush Warehouse ★★★★★   Prince Street

1830-31 Now Arnolfini and offices

The front part of the warehouse was built in 1830-1 as warehousing for Acramans, an iron founders. Four years later it was more than doubled in size when the company, renamed Acraman, Bush, Castle and Co., later Bush and Co., entered the tea trade. The architect for both phases was R. S. Pope, using an elevational system

I believe impossible, to find a mill in Manchester or Wigan which is quite so handsome.

After being empty and neglected for many years, in 1975 the warehouse was gutted internally and converted into the Arnolfini Gallery and offices by the J T Building Group, under their company architect Roger Mortimer. In order to make the economics work they needed to add a floor. To people who admired the building (though many fewer admired it then than now) it

he had successfully developed for his 1828 Wool Hall and other buildings. He was a highly skilled designer of classical buildings and it is remarkable that such a man was able to evolve this equally attractive and very economical industrial style. However, when the Bush warehouse is looked at carefully it is obviously the work of a classicist, but one who could do without all the apparatus of columns and pediments, and was prepared to build in Bristol's cheapest material, the local grey Pennant sandstone. He transformed this usually depressing material by using Bath stone dressings. I can think of only one other man who had similar (though greater) skills, his older contemporary the great Prussian architect Karl Friedrich Schinkel.

The Bush Warehouse occupies one of the most commanding sites in the City Docks, at the point where the two arms of the Floating Harbour meet, and is big enough to impose its presence on these great stretches of water. It is worth remembering that though exceptionally big in Bristol, it is quite small by Lancashire standards, but also worth realising that it would be hard,

threatened to be a disaster. It turned out to be the very opposite, a triumph, the classic answer to people who say that it is impossible to make satisfactory additions to a great building without imitating its style. The inclined glass structure makes the perfect cap on a much loved building, now almost unthinkable without it.

The renovation of the Bush warehouse and its occupation by Arnolfini was the first major move into Bristol's abandoned dockside. For a long time it seemed that no others would follow, but slowly they did. It can now be seen as the start of the transformation of the docks from a wasteland into the wonderland they are today: the most significant physical change in Bristol since the wartime bombing. The power of a successful art gallery or similar cultural building to rejuvenate a neglected area was first demonstrated by the Arnolfini. It is the direct ancestor of the Guggenheim at Bilbao and now countless others. Its historic importance is incalculable, and despite appearing on a commemorative postage stamp, has not been sufficiently recognised.

Brunel House ★ St George's Road
1837-9 Now occupied by the City Planning Department

Brunel House started life as the Royal Western Hotel. Brunel originally wanted his railway terminus to be positioned just north of the cathedral so that it would be in the heart of the city and conveniently close to the docks. He had the hotel built in St George's Road so that passengers who had arrived in Bristol by his trains could stay there before going on to New York by his ship. After the hotel was built it was found impossible to drive the railway line expensively into the city and Brunel had to be content with a terminus at Temple Meads, leaving the hotel rather high and dry. That splendidly romantic story has been doubted, though it's difficult to see any other reason for building a hotel in this rather hidden-away location. What is certainly true is that the building was one of the earliest hotels. Railways disgorged passengers in numbers that the old coaching inns couldn't accommodate, so a new building type had to be invented.

The hotel was built in 1837-9 to the design of the Bristol architect Richard Shackleton Pope. Its original interiors have long disappeared, so only the curious four-storey façade survives. It consists of a recessed centre with projecting end pavilions with great archways allowing carriage access to stabling at the back. The pavilions are linked by a long colonnade of twelve very expensive two-storey-high Ionic columns. A somewhat inaccurate lithograph in the City Art Gallery shows that the hotel's entrance was a modest little doorway in the centre, dwarfed by this enormous colonnade. It is hard to see what purpose it serves, except to look sumptuous. There is very little that can be said in favour of this façade. I can't do better than quote Timothy Mowl –

> Brunel is supposed to have worked together with Pope on the design, an unlikely combination, but the four-storey elevation does give the impression that one architect designed the top two storeys while the other, with little reference to his partner, prepared the bottom two.

Although Pope was a poor designer of Gothic buildings he was a more than competent designer of classical ones, so it is possible that Brunel did interfere by demanding at a late stage that the colonnade should be added to a design which otherwise was more or less fixed. Nonetheless, although it doesn't stand up to any sort of critical analysis, in its context, this great row of Grecian columns, longer even than those in the Victoria Rooms' portico, is a splendid thing.

The hotel was not a success. Having opened in 1839 it closed sixteen years later.

Clifton Suspension Bridge ★★★★★

1836-64

More has been written about the Suspension Bridge than any other building or structure in Bristol. There is nothing new to discover or to say.

The 23-year-old Brunel made several submissions to a competition held in 1829 to find a design for the Clifton bridge. They were condemned by the far more experienced Thomas Telford for having spans too great to be practical. Next year there was another competition, which Brunel won with a design with a reduced span of 630 feet. He achieved this by proposing a large projecting abutment on the Somerset side. The pylons to support the chains were to be covered in iron plates cast with ancient Egyptian motifs. His estimate of £52,000 was more than the money available and caused a delay until 1836 when work began. The two abutments and the cores of the pylons were built and the chains forged by 1843, but

by then the estimate had risen to £70,000 and work stopped, apparently for ever. In 1853 the chains were sold and in 1859 Brunel died. In 1861 the Royal Institution of Civil Engineers encouraged the setting up of a new company to complete the bridge as a memorial to Brunel. The two great railway engineers, Hawkshaw and Barlow, were appointed, and work began again. As Brunel's Hungerford Suspension Bridge was then being

dismantled, its chains were purchased and elongated by additional links and put in place. To save money (and improve the design, though that was not the intention) the Egyptian flim-flam was omitted. The bridge was opened in 1864, at that time leading from Clifton to nowhere in particular. It is an extraordinarily beautiful thing, and in that setting one of the great sights of England. (Imagine the uproar if somebody suggested doing it today.)

In the second half of the nineteenth century Brunel was not a hero in Bristol's board rooms. There he was remembered for his hopelessly optimistic cost estimates, for the failure of his pneumatic railway, his broad gauge that had to be converted at enormous cost to standard gauge, and the revolutionary ships that never fulfilled what he promised for them. Hundreds of people in Bristol had lost the money they had invested in his enterprises. John Latimer, Bristol's greatest historian, seldom showed emotion in his writing, but his 1887 comments on Brunel blister the page. Cost over-runs and failed projects are ultimately forgotten, but successes survive to be enjoyed and recognised. Brunel is now, quite rightly,

the great hero, even the symbol, of nineteenth-century engineering and enterprise, certainly helped by that marvellous photograph of him in his scruffy trousers and stove pipe hat, nonchalantly smoking his cigar.

I wrote at the beginning that there is nothing new to say about the bridge. There is perhaps one little point which, as far as I am aware, the historians have missed. Professor Pugsley, who held the chair of Engineering at Bristol University in the 1960s, and was, I believe, the consultant for the Bridge, told me that when Barlow made his designs for the re-used Hungerford Bridge chains, he made a small error in his calculations. As a result, the last few suspension rods at each end are slightly too long. Instead of being in tension, as they should be, they are in compression. If some wicked person were to attack them with a hacksaw, instead of parting with a ping, they would simply close up as though nothing had happened.

Brunel's Temple Meads Station ★★★★★

Temple Way

1840-41

Temple Meads is the oldest surviving railway terminus in the world.

Whilst Brunel was working in Bristol on the City docks and the Suspension Bridge (q.v.), he so impressed a group of business men who wanted to build a railway to London that they appointed him to be the engineer of what became the Great Western Railway Company. In 1840 they opened the line from Bristol to Bath and in the following year to London. The Company had two offices and two Boards of Directors, one of each in Bristol and Paddington. The Bristol office, the first to be built and the only original one to survive, was designed by the Bristol architect R. S. Pope, working in some sort of collaboration with Brunel. His façade, in an uninspiring Tudor style, is intact except that it has lost the gateway on its left which matched the surviving one on the right. Inside, the Board Room and the Company Secretary's office survive.

The train shed, also surviving miraculously in nearly complete condition, was designed by Brunel, with Pope presumably contributing the dull exterior and a few of the architectural details inside. Track level is 12 feet above ground in order to allow trains to bridge the Floating Harbour immediately outside the station, so the shed was raised to that level by being built above its ticket office, waiting rooms, stables etc., as well as over a wide underpass which allowed vehicles and pedestrians to get from side to side without having to cross the tracks.

The roof of the train shed is supported on rows of cast-iron columns which run along the front of the platforms on each side, making them something like the aisles in a church. Between the platforms there were five broad-gauge tracks uninterrupted by further columns, so the span of the roof was exceptionally wide – 317 feet. Along both sides of the roof is a series of timber pendants and arched timbers supporting them. They are imitation hammer beams, intended to give a respectably medieval feel to the roof, but serving no structural function. The real structure is much more interesting. It consists of a series of gently arched timber beams resting at about a fifth of their span on supporting columns, which act as pivots over which they would rotate unless fixed. At the slightly pointed apex of the roof, where they would drop, they lean upon and support each other; at the bottom,

The train shed as was, from Bourne's *History and Description of the Great Western Railway*, 1843

where they would lift, they are tied down to the ground. This highly ingenious and economical balancing act means that the roof requires no ties to prevent the feet of the arches from spreading. It was enormously admired, and although greater spans were to be achieved later, remains an awesome and beautiful achievement.

At the rear of the train shed, backing onto the offices, a short length of the building has a low flat ceiling above which were drawing offices etc. supported by columns between the tracks. When trains arrived at the station their locomotives pulled into this end of the shed, were uncoupled and transferred to an adjoining track by an ingenious mechanism called a sector table. They then reversed out, ready to be transferred to their original track and re-coupled to their carriages for the return to London.

There have been huge additions and extensions to the original station, some of great interest, but this account is concerned only with Brunel's epoch-making terminus. Its historical importance cannot be over-estimated, nor the wonder that it has survived so completely. The only regret is that Brunel's goods depot to the north of the passenger station has been destroyed.

Christ Church, Clifton ★★★

Clifton Down Road
1841-4, 1859, 1885

Christ Church was one of the many churches throughout the history of Christianity which had to be built bit by bit over a long period of time as the necessary funds became available. For Christ Church they were raised by subscriptions and a church rate, and accumulated slowly because no big benefactor emerged.

The body of the church was built in 1841-4 to the design of Charles Dyer. He was born and brought up in Bristol and got the bulk of his work here, but practised in London. He designed splendid classical buildings, such as the Victoria Rooms (q.v.), and dull Gothic ones, so he could have been a bad choice since in the 1840s churches more or less had to be Gothic. However, for Christ Church he built a splendid large nave and two transepts but no aisles. He probably became ill during the building work because an architect called Ewan Christian was brought in to finish it, presumably to Dyer's design. Since three other architects were eventually employed it is difficult to be sure which work is Dyer's, but it seems that he must have been responsible for the dull interior and the magnificent exterior of the transepts, north porch and lower stage of the tower, all in the Early English style. He died, aged only 54, in 1848.

Ten years later, another tranche of money having accumulated, the vicar wanted to use it to increase accommodation by building aisles. The congregation, putting appearances before utility, voted against them and demanded that the tower should be completed. It would be fascinating to know their motive; was it civic pride or Church of England triumphalism – getting one over on the dissenters and the Catholics, who were particularly unpopular at that time? I suspect it was more probably sectarian pride, one in the eye for the Ritualists down the hill at All Saints' in Pembroke Road. Whichever, they appointed John Norton to complete the tower and build a spire. He was an out-and-out Gothicist (Tyntesfield, Holy Trinity Stapleton, etc) and his steeple, undoubtedly his masterpiece, is the feature which makes Christ Church one of the glories of Clifton.

Dyer had placed three blind arches on each face of the stump of tower. Norton repeated them on the new stages, making them progressively taller up to the bell stage at the top, where they are real arches filled by louvres. He also continued Dyer's angle buttresses, fading them out just before the top of the tower, thus beginning to taper its silhouette. He continued the taper by chamfering the four corners to accept four little spirelets at the base of the main spire, and set high pointed window openings between them. This junction between tower and spire (always the difficult bit) is thus made smooth and inevitable-seeming: a resounding success. Twenty-six years later, in 1885, the fourth and last architect, W. Basset-Smith, finally built the aisles and completed the church. Through all this time and change of architects the same Early English style was employed and only the sharpest eyes can now detect that Christ Church was not built in one go by one architect. It is a thoroughbred designed by a committee.

Victoria Rooms and fountains ★★★★

Queen's Road

1842, 1911-17

The Victoria Rooms were opened on the Queen's birthday in 1842, paid for by a 'committee of leading citizens' to be a Conservative and more exclusive alternative to the Clifton Assembly Rooms (q.v.). Their architect was Charles Dyer. He produced the most imposing classical building in Bristol, with the only octostyle (eight-columned) portico. It makes a fascinating comparison with Sir Robert Smirke's slightly earlier British Museum portico, which is also octostyle, though much bigger. Dyer's portico sings in its happy proportions: Smirke's shouts, somehow managing to be louder but duller. The Victoria Rooms is Charles Dyer's finest building.

The beautiful pediment sculpture is worth closer examination than it usually gets. Its subject (the Graces accompanying Athena the Goddess of Wisdom being driven in her chariot) is, and always was, less important than the flurry of draperies and galloping hooves rushing from right to left. It was carved by a local mason to

the design of the brilliant young sculptor Musgrave Lewthwaite Watson, who died five years after the Rooms were opened.

Perhaps because of their exclusiveness, the Rooms were never very successful and in 1920 were bought by a member of the Wills family and given to the University for use by the Students' Union. In the 1930s the interior was gutted by fire and rebuilt in a cheap and singularly dreary manner. In 1965 the students moved to new premises, and the Rooms never really found a purpose until the Music Department moved in, which seems an admirable use, if only they wouldn't disfigure the portico with their tasteless advertising banners.

In the intensely imperialist atmosphere of 1910 it was inevitable that upon Edward VII's death another committee of leading citizens should decide to commission a memorial, which they decided to locate in front of the Victoria Rooms. On the advice of the Royal Institute of British Architects they appointed the brilliant

Edwin Rickards, of Lanchester and Rickards, architects of the Central Hall in Westminster and the glorious Cardiff City Hall. It was probably no coincidence that the competition for the statue was then won by Henry Poole, as he had worked successfully with Rickards on several earlier buildings. It was a wonderful partnership – the best architect of the currently fashionable land-of-hope-and-glory baroque, and one of the best of a notably brilliant generation of British sculptors. After the Committee had

seen the statue they agreed that Rickard and Poole should again work together to produce a fountain.

The statue of the king in his garter robes was necessarily conventional, but it is a great deal more splendid than most municipal statues. (He is made to seem taller, and therefore slimmer, than he was in reality by the old portraitists' trick of giving him a disproportionately small head.) The beautifully patinated green bronze figure is greatly enhanced by its high stone plinth, with a glorious cascade of typically Rickardian mouldings at its base. But the glory of the monument is the wonderful baroque fountain, one of the finest in the country, with its mermaids sporting amongst sea creatures and great fronds of seaweed. Sculpturally it is second in Bristol only to Rysbrack's equestrian William III in Queen Square, but much more fun. Rickards and Poole, like Edward VII, were enthusiastic and frequent visitors to the fleshly delights of belle époque Paris, and in a way their joyous fountain is probably the King's truest monument.

Bank of England ★★★★★   Broad Street
1844-6

The former Bristol branch of the Bank of England is the one supremely great Greek Revival building in Bristol, and among the best in England. It was built in 1844-6 to the design of C. R. Cockerell. He had made important archaeological discoveries in Greece and was Professor of Architecture at the Royal Academy, yet he was one of

the least pedantic and most inventive architects of the nineteenth century. At a time when the Gothic Revival was sweeping the country he spent his life demonstrating the power of the classical tradition, and how it could be developed. He was the classical architect's classical architect. His buildings have none of the easily appreciated drama and decoration of Gothic ones. To those who have not caught the classical infection they seem reserved and dry. They will never be widely popular, as, say, Bristol University's tower is popular.

It would take many pages to explain all the clever and original details in Cockerell's tiny Bank of England façade. I must select only two or three, and ask the reader to follow my words by continual reference back to the photograph. The dominating features are the Greek Doric columns, supporting, as Doric columns must, the Doric entablature which runs under the iron balcony. There are only two columns, and two flat-faced pilasters. (Orthodox.) The pilasters have caps which are slightly moulded. These mouldings then continue, not as the tops of columns or pilasters but as the bottom mouldings of the entablature. (Unorthodox.) Where the entablature meets the channelled end walls it becomes their entablature. Now note a tiny bit of drama. Throughout the width of the façade the cornice projects the usual few inches from the face of the entablature, but when it turns towards the street at each end it projects much more, so much that it has to have a little bracket underneath to support it. (Very unorthodox.) The effect is extraordinarily dynamic. (Very, very unorthodox – classical architecture was supposed to be calm, static.) I could go on: nobody, for example, had ever turned a wide projecting entablature into a balcony, complete with iron railings. (Nobody but the Professor would have dared to. The Doric order comes from the Parthenon, the architects' Holy of Holies.)

Another, more prominent, feature probably surprised the Bristol architects as much as those tiny ones. Orthodoxy dictated that where there was a pediment it sat on its entablature; the two were considered to be one. Here they are separated by a whole storey and its windows. In fact this was not new; it had been done by that great breaker of rules, Robert Adam, way back in the previous century. In the 1840s going back to the Adam brothers was itself unorthodox: at that period they were as unfashionable and despised as tower blocks are today.

Cockerell was a giant, but he lived at a time when the classical tradition to which he devoted his life had only a few decades left to it. Technological change was inevitably going to require a new sort of architecture, which duly arrived. And yet … Classical architectural forms go back more than 2500 years. They are older than the great religions of the world. They grew up as our civilisation grew, carrying a weight of symbolism and memory which no other built forms, anywhere, have ever acquired. They endured the long medieval centuries when they were forgotten, but they came back. Who can be certain that this time they have gone for ever?

12 and 13 Buckingham Vale ★★★★

c1845

These, the most beautiful semi-detached houses in Bristol, and among the most beautiful anywhere, were almost certainly designed by the highly gifted and adaptable Bristol architect Richard Shackleton Pope, and were built in about 1845. Pope, who had a very large practice, designed many dull Gothic buildings (e.g. the Guildhall and the offices of Temple Meads station q.v.), some lovely classical ones as well as this pair, and a few classically-based but ornament-free industrial ones (the Wool Hall, Bush Warehouse q.v.). This pair of houses is fascinating for several reasons.

Many architects wrestled with the problem of how to fit a house, with all its windows and chimneys, into a version of a Greek or Roman temple. We, of course, can see that the idea was absurd, but for at least three centuries people thought differently. We can, however, see that some of their attempts were extraordinarily beautiful (so perhaps our opinion isn't worth much). At Buckingham Vale Pope (assuming it was he) used an idea he had used earlier at his church of St Mary-on-the-Quay. This was to treat the accommodation, or at least the front part of it, as a visually separate block running parallel to the street, and to straddle it with the 'temple', running at right angles to it. At Buckingham Vale the fronts of the houses seem to slide under the temple: a logical and most attractive concept.

Several of the eighteenth-century entries in this book refer to the rules of classical architectural composition. Many rules, particularly during the Palladian period, were absurd, with no other justification than fashion.

Most, however, were based on the fact that some things look better than others, and that untalented designers produce better buildings if they are given simple rules to follow. One of the most basic was that in a symmetrical composition – and most classical buildings were symmetrical – it looks best if there is something in the centre on which the eye can focus. So in a terrace of houses, for example, there should be an odd number of them so that the central one can be balanced equally on either side. In a house façade there should be an odd number of windows, for the same reason. If you knew this simple rule, and craftsmen often didn't, you couldn't go too far wrong. But what about a pair of semis – which after about 1800 became increasingly popular? If they are to be of equal size they will have an equal number of windows, and that means they can't have a central one, which in any case would be on the line of the party wall. Architects got over that by putting a niche or something similar in the centre, or dodged the problem altogether by making the houses of different design. At Buckingham Vale Pope had decided or been told to provide two identical houses and had the additional problem posed by his 'temple'. Two thousand five hundred years ago architects discovered that a short colonnade with a central column looked worse than one with a central gap, because the gaps, being shadowed, are more telling than the paler columns. So they evolved the rule that colonnades must have an even number of columns, and if they were short, looked best if the central gap was slightly wider than the others. Pope's temple front therefore had to have four (or more) columns, preferably with a wider gap between the two inner columns than the two outer ones. However he found that if he did that, each of the central columns would come immediately in front of a window. He could either move the windows sideways, which would position them inconveniently in the rooms, or he could break the rule and move the columns closer together. He put convenience before orthodoxy and moved the columns. It had an interesting result. The coupled columns, because they are close together, act visually as the orthodox central gap would have done: they give the necessary central focus. No doubt his more stupid colleagues were shocked because they knew the rule but not its rationale. I can't

offhand recall any other building where this was done. It gives a curious twist, the jolt of the unexpected, to this strange, beautiful pair of houses.

Another thing about these houses is particularly admirable. How often have we seen otherwise delightful semis or terraces ripped apart by their visually illiterate owners having painted them in different colours, sometimes even with the dividing line painted down the centre of a pilaster? Here the two householders sensibly work as one. They deserve our gratitude.

All the other houses in this short street of taller and less spectacular semis must be by Pope because they all play similar tricks with their pilasters. In these he groups the two pilasters at the ends of each pair to enclose the entrances. This hidden-away street is one of Clifton's lesser-known treasures.

The Clifton Lido ★★★★

1850, 2008

The Clifton Victoria Baths, designed by the splendid and ubiquitous Richard Shackleton Pope, were opened in July 1850, at a time when few houses had bathrooms, and several decades before municipal washing and swimming baths were opened anywhere in England. It was operated by a company that offered:

> private baths for the convenience of ladies and gentlemen, a medicated bath for the use of invalids, and a spacious plunging and swimming bath.

Admission and two towels was a shilling (5p), children half price.

Apparently the venture was not profitable because in the 1870s a chunk of the building was sold and converted into a pub, and in 1880 the pool was sold to another company. They also failed to prosper, going into voluntary liquidation in 1897. The pool was then bought by Bristol Corporation, at that time engaged on a programme of building public baths. Things went well for nearly a century, until 1990 when the Corporation, then engaged on a programme of closing public baths, discovered a convenient leak and promptly closed the

pool. After a year or two a campaign began to save the building, reaching a climax in 1997 when the Council gave a housing association permission to demolish most of it and build flats and houses on the site. The turning point came in 1998 when the pool was listed, long after it should have been. It was then bought by Arne Ringner, of the very successful Glass Boat Company, and after a two-million-pound revamp by the Bristol architects Marshall and Kendon, reopened in 2008.

Externally the façade consists of two short wings and a centrepiece with an Egyptian doorway (a curious stylistic choice for a building depending on a copious supply of water). It now suffers from its rather sad pub-half having been altered and painted, whilst the beautifully restored pool-half is unpainted Bath stone. Behind the façade the architects were faced by a collapsing interior consisting of a row of dilapidated wooden changing cubicles along one side, and an empty and derelict two-storey structure on the other. Almost all of this, irrespective of its date, was retained and restored. The changing cubicles, for example, were completely dismantled, repaired, and put back together, and each of them was given its own shower. All the new work on the other hand was deliberately constructed of visibly modern materials. Where, for example, the old beams were insufficient, they were strengthened by undisguised steel stiffening.

Lidos everywhere are under threat because the expense of heating and treating water has become so great. They can survive only by offering much more than a swim. Here the economics are supported by treatment rooms, a bar, and a high quality restaurant. Costs are reduced by a sophisticated heating system depending on 720 solar collectors on the roof, as well as by other devices, both to gain and retain heat. An imaginative educational feature is a large gauge in the restaurant which displays the collectors' changing power output.

Internally, the scene is entirely modern, the two-storey restaurant being enclosed by glass through which all the original structure and handrails remain visible. The pool is spectacular. Instead of the usual arrangement where the water level is below the surrounding walkway, here it is raised so that the water is not far below the eye level of people sitting beside the pool. The water flows gently over the precisely level rim into a grating running around the pool, so that the effect is a great sheet of water raised above the floor. It is a magical sight.

The Lido is included here for three reasons: first for its quality as an 1850 building, for which it would perhaps merit two stars; secondly as an outstanding example of how the enthusiasm of a few active and intelligent people can overcome bureaucratic obstruction and lack of imagination, and thirdly for the sheer quality of the conversion, for which it merits four stars.

Lloyds Bank ★★★★ Corn Street

1857 Formerly the West of England Bank

At the end of the eighteenth century and in the early years of the nineteenth there were bank failures in almost every town, so the Victorian banks needed to reassure customers that they held huge financial reserves and were of impregnable solidity and respectability. They believed the best way was to build solid and respectable buildings, and the richer they appeared the more reassuring they would be. In Corn Street the banks used architecture competitively to proclaim their success and the depths of their reserves. When the West of England Bank decided in 1854 to leave the cramped premises they rented in the Exchange and build their own premises opposite, they thought that the best architect to win the competition on their behalf was William Bruce Gingell. They gave him a blank cheque and told him to flaunt their wealth as magnificently as he could. In architectural terms magnificence, impreg-

The original façade [Reece Winstone Collection]

nable solidity and respectability meant classical. Gothic was respectable, but it savoured too much of hymn books and penniless curates: classical suggested ducal palaces and the riches of Midas, king of Phrygia. But clearly it had to be the richest classical that money could buy. The richest classical building then admired was Sansovino's Library in the Piazzetta at Venice.

The bank was opened in 1857. For its design Gingell had taken Sansovino's Library as his starting point, but he developed it to produce something quite different and original. The ground floor of the Library is an open arcade with its arches supported on piers, and with big Doric columns superimposed on the piers to support the entablature running across the building. Gingell followed that pattern, but enriched it by putting a smaller column and arch within the big arch, and replacing Sansovino's Doric entablature with a great frieze of sculpture. He beefed up the smaller columns by running each one through three cubic blocks (a sixteenth-century motif), but Doric columns are meant to be thick and chunky, and these are absurdly skinny. Why? – because if they were thicker there would be no room for the blocks. Does it matter? – not in the least because they and the blocks do what they were intended to do – fill space. On the first floor Gingell followed Sansovino more closely, but he built a bigger and richer sculpted frieze. The effect of these changes (and others) was more profound than it sounds. The resulting façade is crammed with incident so that the biggest plain surfaces are the panes of glass in the windows, but everything is powerfully controlled by the vertical columns and the great horizontal friezes. What could so easily have been a chaos is a wonderful classical balance.

A major element in this is the sculpture. If Gingell had been designing a generation earlier he would have required the carving to be in much lower relief, but a revolution in taste had occurred and he had it cut so deeply that it is almost free-standing. John Thomas, the sculptor, probably suggested the iconography – Art, Industry, Commerce, Navigation, Prudence etc – but there can be no doubt that the deeply shadowed carving had been an essential part of Gingell's instructions to him. The sculpture is hugely enjoyable. It is that curious sub-branch of the art, decorative sculpture, none of it quite good enough to stand on its own in an art gallery, but technically brilliant and wonderfully good at doing what was required of it, enriching a building. In fact Thomas probably carved little of it, or possibly none at all. He was enormously busy at the time with commissions all over the country, and was still controlling the entire sculptural programme of the Houses of Parliament and carving much of it himself. For Gingell's bank he probably made some preliminary drawings and left the rest to what must have been the Bristol squad in an army of highly competent assistants.

Sansovino's façade is very long; 20 bays: Gingell's was only five. Sansovino's Library has no obvious entrance

architect, who took such care not to damage Gingell's concept, should have mangled it in this way: I don't know, but I can hazard a guess. After more than half a century of nineteenth century smoke, the façade would have been black. The architect saw some Portland appearing through the murk and assumed that everything was Portland. It was not until 1974 when the façade was cleaned that all was revealed. Weathering since then has dulled the contrast, but in any case it doesn't seem to matter much because the texture of the building is more important than its colour. The alterations were managed well and the elongated façade is splendid, but Gingell's original five symmetrical bays were better. His façade was smaller but more concentrated, more powerful.

The vast banking hall inside 'this pecuniary palace' is flaunting carried to the ultimate, but it is now let down by the graceless modern furnishings and security screens. However, what really matters is the glorious façade: a stunning achievement which still evokes gasps when architecture-loving visitors are taken to see it. So: did this hugely expensive display of success and financial stability work? For a few years it seemed that it did, but in 1878 the bank became bankrupt, having been cooking

because its doorway is out of sight inside the arcade: Gingell's bank had its entrance very prominently in the centre bay (see facing page). Early in the twentieth century the façade was extended by the addition of an extra bay on the left containing a new entrance, and the old entrance was converted into a window to match the others. Great care was taken to fit the new entrance respectfully into Gingell's façade, but it had a curious defect: the new work was carried out in white Portland stone, whilst the old is in golden Bath stone and only the sculpture is in Portland stone. I don't know why the

the books for years. The primary reason, as ever, was that they had made imprudent loans, in this case to a couple of companies, and had then pumped in more and more money in an attempt to rescue the situation. But possibly it was also because they spent just a bit too much on trumpeting wealth they didn't really have.

In 1892 the last remaining assets, including this building, were bought by Lloyds Bank. The West of England Bank's directors had hurt a lot of investors when they fell, but they left us a treasure beyond price.

Foster's Almshouse ★★★★   Colston Street
1861, 1883

John Foster founded his almshouse in 1483, with a little chapel dedicated to the Three Kings of Cologne attached to it. Under the administration of the Corporation in 1702 everything except the chapel was demolished and rebuilt. In 1835 the government reformed all the old corporations, and independent trustees in each town were appointed to take responsibility for the almshouses. In 1861 the Bristol trustees decided to rebuild Foster's again and this time to restore the chapel, which alone survives from 1483. As their architects they appointed Foster and Wood, who were rebuilding the Trinity Almshouse in Old Market in a style closely modelled on the mid-fifteenth-century hospital at Beaune in Burgundy, which was much admired in England at that time. It was clearly enjoyed by the trustees as well, because they instructed Foster and Wood to use the same style for Foster's Almshouse.

Work proceeded in stages over 22 years as money became available, being completed in 1883. Money wasn't skimped, as the profusion of turrets, oriels, domes, gables and finials demonstrate. All these and the cheerfully diapered walls and roofs are designed with such confidence and brio, and built with such consummate craftsmanship, that this is one of the most enjoyable of Bristol's Victorian buildings.

Writers have occasionally questioned whether some of the money for Foster's wouldn't have been better spent on improved accommodation for the alms-people. That is judging unhistorically. The trustees, typical Victorians, felt that some of the money, since it was earned in Bristol, should be spent on improving Bristol. We can only thank the Gods that they did.

Perry's Carriage Works ★★★ Stokes Croft

1862   Derelict

This listed building, now derelict and long abandoned, is backed by the tall concrete skeleton of its 1960s extension. The City Council has devoted considerable resources to the area's rejuvenation, but has not yet found a developer prepared to take on the expense of rehabilitating this building.

The Carriage Works was designed in 1862 by the 29-year-old E. W. Godwin, who began his career in Bristol, his native city. He had become nationally known in 1861 when he won the competition for Northampton Town Hall. When in 1865 he won the competition for Bristol's new Guildhall he was deprived of the commission when R. S. Pope informed the Corporation of his liaison with the beautiful and married young actress Ellen Terry. He left for London where he was able to live with Terry, fathering Edward Gordon Craig, and becoming a prominent figure in the aesthetic circles of Wilde and Whistler. Today he is best known and admired for his innovative and hugely influential furniture designs.

It is probable that there were never any notable interi-

ors in this industrial and commercial building. The carefully ordered façade consisted of open haulingways on the ground floor which acted as a heavy arcaded base, two upper floors of large arched windows, and a heavy cornice. In the 1850s and '60s there were many façades of this type in Bristol, one or two very closely similar, though probably not by Godwin. His Stokes Croft façade was perhaps the best of the bunch, but not original. It is his subsequent fame which has made it one of the best known of what John Summerson called (not accurately in this case) Bristol Byzantine architecture.

Early in the twentieth century the front of the building was spoilt when the open haulingways along its ground floor were converted into windows set nearly flush with the face of the stonework, thus destroying the necessary depth and weight of the arcade. These have now been boarded up.

[Reece Winstone Collection]

Victoria Square ★★★★   Clifton
1835, 1853, 1863, 1869

Victoria Square happened by accident. In 1835 a speculator called Samuel Hemming built a terrace of houses on land which he had leased from the Society of Merchant Venturers (owners of much of Clifton and Hotwells). His terrace, called Lansdown Place, now forms the Square's north-east side. In 1837 a man who

out and planted. They then fell into their customary torpor until, ten years later in 1863, they persuaded a builder called John Yalland to build a terrace on the south-west side, which he called, rather, pedestrianly, Victoria Square West. Unfortunately his sales went slowly, almost certainly because the age of the posh

had a lease on a field to the south-west of the terrace announced that he was going to build some houses on it. Some alert Merchant, or perhaps one of the Society's advisers, realised that an opportunity had arisen. There was a new and young Queen on the throne, the long years of financial depression were over, and house sales were booming again. The field and all the adjacent land, as well as the site of Hemmings's terrace, was flat – the perfect place to build a square. So the Merchants, acting with untypical promptness, immediately bought the land and built what is now the north-west side of Victoria Square. Before their building was finished in 1853 they had the central garden and its diagonal path laid

terrace house was over. Detached or paired houses with big gardens were now what prosperous people wanted, as the building-up of Pembroke Road, for example, demonstrated. So the Merchants commissioned plans for five substantial detached houses on the remaining side of the Square. They were begun in 1869 and completed in the following year. Two or three years later the last houses in Yalland's terrace were finished, finally completing the Square almost 40 years after it was begun.

So, what of the architecture? The first of the terraces, Lansdown Place, is of rather dim quality, looking back for most of its inspiration to Clifton's Georgian terraces, and with only a few details, such as the unifying line of continuous balconies rather than the earlier separate ones, showing the change in architectural taste which was then taking place. It was designed by Foster and Sons, the excellent architectural practice which, as Foster and Wood, was to dominate Bristol's architecture throughout the rest of the nineteenth century.

The second terrace, Royal Promenade (opposite), is another matter. When it was emerging from its scaffolding it must have been breathtakingly spectacular, the most extreme contrast to what had gone before in Clifton. Royal York Crescent, for example, is simply a row of hundreds of identical windows and dozens of nearly identical balconies set in a plain stuccoed wall. The Promenade is a palace of golden Bath stone. It would be pointless to analyse its composition in any detail, but basically it consists of a large projecting centrepiece, long wings, and projecting pavilions at each end. It is an extremely clever design, not least because it achieves palatial richness without using the Georgian architects' always reliable trick of columns and pediment. The dominating forms are the three long horizontal lines – the cast-iron railings along the back of the pavement, the continuous heavy stone balconies, and the enormously powerful cornice. A detail which gives me constant delight is the continuous row of tiny arched windows above the cornice on the wings and end pavilions (lighting servants' attics). The architects were almost certainly Foster and Wood again.

The rest is anti-climax. Yalland's Victoria Square West, probably designed by Foster and Wood, is splendid but after their fireworks on the adjacent side, seems a trifle tame. Nonetheless, it is well worth studying, particularly in the morning when the sun is on it. The six houses on the fourth side, now somewhat blighted by the continuous traffic running past them, are pleasant but not much more.

Victoria Square is not an architectural unity, but having a mass of large trees in its centre this is seldom worryingly apparent. The memory one carries away is of large trees, wide pavements, and the glorious Royal Promenade.

Former Museum and Library ★★★
Queen's Road
1867-72 Now Browns Restaurant

In 1851 Ruskin published the first volume of his *Stones of Venice*. I cannot think of any other book on architecture, in any language, which made such a colossal and instant impact. An enormous part of its explosive power came from its majestic prose. Here are the opening two paragraphs:

> Since first the dominion of men was asserted over the ocean, three thrones, of mark beyond all others, have been set upon its sands: the thrones of Tyre, Venice, and England. Of the First of these great powers only the memory remains; of the Second the ruin; the Third which inherits their greatness, if we forget their example, may be led through prouder eminence to less pitied destruction.
>
> The exaltation, the sin, and the punishment of Tyre have been recorded for us, in perhaps the most touching words ever uttered by the Prophets of Israel against the cities of the stranger. But we read them as a lovely song; and close our ears to the sternness of their warning: for the very depth of the Fall of Tyre has blinded us to its reality, and we forget, as we watch the bleaching of the rocks between the sunshine and the sea, that they were once 'As in Eden, the garden of God.'

It wasn't only architects who were swept along that wonderful torrent of words: almost every literate person was carried away; and not only in Britain. In France, for example, Marcel Proust acknowledged Ruskin as his greatest influence. In Bristol the flood was irresistible and took years to recede. Here, the best example of pure Venetian Gothic is the Museum and Library, built in 1867-72, by the architect John Foster, working, for this job only, with Archibald Ponton, who was then designing the Granary on Welsh Back (q.v.) in a more original version of the style.

It is said that the plans were designed by Ponton and the elevations by Foster: an almost impossible arrangement which must have been forced on them by some circumstance of which I am ignorant. (It happened also at the nearby Royal West of England Academy (q.v.) when, after a competition, the Academicians liked the plans of one man and the front elevation of another. The result was a disaster which had to be corrected, at great

expense, later.) However as originally designed, Foster's façade was a glorious riot of open arcades, stone balconies, polychromatic brick and stone, and sculpture. The budget put paid to most of that, and wartime bombing destroyed the great parapet and cornice, the carved figures and the delightful little canopies at each corner of the parapet. The building was converted into a refectory in 1949. Victorian architecture being then considered contemptible, what was left of the interior was more or less gutted and the outer bays of the colonnade walled-in. The façade is now a ghost, though a friendly and attractive one. The return wall on University Road was relatively undamaged and is now the best part, though much too often ignored.

Avon Insurance Building ★★★

51 Broad Street

1868 Now a restaurant and offices

Before the 1940s bombing the central districts of all British cities had dozens of small Victorian commercial buildings of this general type, most of them, as here, built on the site of a single earlier house. In this case the house would have been Georgian and itself probably a replacement of a replacement; a series of rebuildings going back to Bristol's earliest years. Throughout this process the width of the frontage would usually have remained the same, though some of the earlier houses would not necessarily have occupied the full width. Many had narrow alleys at the side leading originally to the garden, but from quite early in the medieval period, gardens in such tightly crowded areas within the town walls were often converted to courts of tiny cottages. The cottages have all gone, but several of Broad Street's medieval alleys remain to this day.

In the 1860s intending builders had two broad styles to choose from, Gothic or classical. Most businessmen had not had the classical education which might have tempted them to lean that way, so for their buildings they preferred the high moral tone associated with Gothic architecture to the low moral tone suggested by the lives of the classical gods and goddesses. So the majority of commercial buildings in this era were Gothic.

The Broad Street office was designed by Ponton and Gough, who were working at around the same time on what has subsequently become one of the most famous High Victorian buildings in Britain, the Granary on Welsh Back (q.v.). The two buildings look very different, but both owe their punch to the same feature: the full thickness of their walls is visible, un-obscured by windows set into their reveals. In the Granary there are no windows at all. In the office building the windows are set back, well behind the columns and arches. This fully revealed wall thickness is a major component of both buildings' visual success. In the Broad Street façade it additionally solved the difficulty which Victorian architects always had to face when designing Gothic buildings – how to put opening windows into small pointed arches without making them look absurd. Here, behind the Gothic screen, they are simply rows of utterly conventional and convenient rectangular sash windows filled with the latest plate glass.

Both buildings are notable for the amount of imagination which went into designing different treatments for each floor. The ground floor of the Broad Street building has piers supporting flat lintels, the first floor has double arches set within three big ones, the second floor has pairs of flat arches set within piers supporting lintels, and the top floor has a continuous row of little arches. The size of the elements decreases up the façade and each row of arches is shorter than the one below it. It is paradoxical that this splendid Gothic façade can be analyzed in these classical terms. Most of even the most ardent Gothicists had been trained in the rules of classical composition.

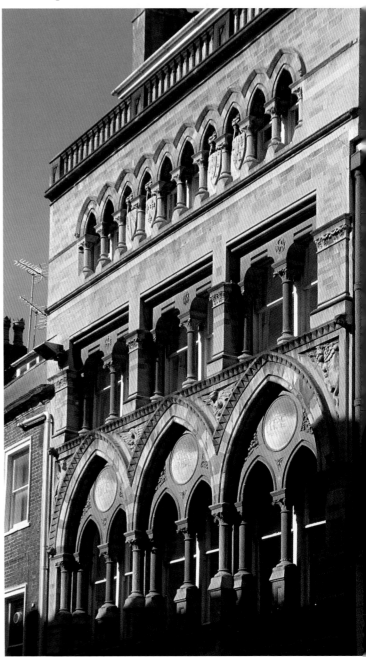

The Granary ★★★★★ Welsh Back

1869 Now converted to flats

In the 1860s, which were boom years in Bristol, the city led the country in the design of commercial, industrial and public buildings. Today it would be very unusual to find a book on Victorian architecture which omitted a photograph of Bristol's finest – the Granary.

It was built in 1869 for Wait, James and Co. William Killigrew Wait was one of those imaginative and dynamic individuals who were so prominent in nineteenth-century local government and are so lacking today. He was one of the initiators of the movement to build the cathedral's nave, and when it got going he paid for its north porch. He was MP for Gloucester, a very early supporter of votes for women and he completed his Granary in the year he became Mayor of Bristol. He chose his architects, Ponton and Gough, with his usual fine judgement. Writers never fail to say how much the Granary was influenced by the writings of John Ruskin: no doubt it was; in 1869 almost every architect in Britain was influenced by him. But Ponton, whose subsequent work reveals that he must have been the designer in the partnership, would have been perfectly aware, as so

many writers are not, that Ruskin's much quoted dictum that ornament is 'the chief part of architecture' is arrant nonsense. Ornament is an attractive dress on the body of architecture, no more, and as the Bush Warehouse (q.v.) shows, the body can be beautiful without clothes. If the unclothed body is not comely, no dress can make it beautiful, it can merely disguise some of its defects. Pugin, who designed the ornament on the Houses of Parliament, got it right. His 'two great rules are 1st, that there should be no features about a building which are not necessary for convenience, construction or propriety; 2nd, that all ornament should consist of enrichment of the essential construction of the building.' I cannot think of a building which exemplifies those rules better than the Granary.

A granary is a complicated piece of machinery, and Ponton's building, first and foremost, was a highly efficient machine. The site was small so the building had to be tall to accommodate all that Wait required. This meant that when it was full of grain the load bearing down on the lower parts of the walls was very great. Fortunately a relatively cheap local material which could accept compressive forces of that kind had recently come on the market, the red and buff Cattybrook machine-made bricks produced near Almondsbury. One of the functions of the granary was to dry the grain. This meant that the external walls had to be as open to the air as possible. The traditional solution, which Ponton adopted, was to build parts of the walls with open-work brick grilles. As these are not strong and can only be used in quite small panels, Ponton put them into arches. Arches were an essential part of the structure because they are stronger and more permanent than the only possible alternative at that time, wooden lintels. The arches transfer the loads they carry from above onto the brick piers between them. The great piers of sheer brickwork at the outer corners of the building serve the visual purpose of framing the lacy detail between them, and give the building its appearance of strength and stability. But this aesthetic role is a by-product of a mechanical necessity: they stiffen the building and house the internal hoists (which in most granaries and maltings were external and therefore subject to rot). On the ground floor there is a series of circular port-holes, now blocked. They enormously enrich the variety of brick patterns, but they also were a necessary part of the working machine – they allowed the shutes which delivered sacks to waiting carts to be poked through them when that was required.

It would have been possible for an architect to have done all this and produce no more than a decently attractive and efficient building, but Ponton was no ordinary architect. The way he varied his grilles with a different pattern on every floor, and varied his arches, some only a single storey in height, some going through two and some three, some round-headed, some pointed, some flat, is wonderfully imaginative. At that period there was a craze for polychromatic as well as patterned brickwork. Ponton mixed red and buff Cattybrook bricks with a little (more expensive) stonework, but one small economy is visible if you look for it. Polychromatic brickwork always looks best if it has a small admixture of black bricks. These came from Staffordshire and were very expensive. Ponton made do by painting some of the red bricks instead.

The problem of finding a new use for this hugely important building became acute half a century ago. After being empty for many years it became a very successful jazz venue, but that only occupied the lower floors. It has now been converted into flats which occupy the whole building other than the ground floor restaurant. The conversion by the architects Barton Willmore is brilliantly successful, managing to change the use without the slightest sign externally that anything is different. They even repainted the black bricks which were losing their original paint.

There is no other building of pierced and polychromatic brickwork, in Bristol or anywhere else, which is the equal of Archibald Ponton's. Now that we can admire Victorian buildings, as our grandparents could not, we can celebrate him.* But let us also honour William Wait who gave us this treasure, and so much else. Today he is entirely forgotten.

* In 1958 Pevsner, in his *North Somerset and Bristol* volume, dismissed the Granary in a short sentence, adding 'but the pleasure of Welsh Back is not its own buildings but Redcliffe Parade in the distance'. A child of his time, he considered the Granary unworthy of illustration. (And yet he was one of the earliest writers to start appreciating Victorian buildings – but not this one. It was simply too extreme, too Victorian.)

Downleaze **★★★★**   Sneyd Park

1891-99

From the 1880s the more forward-looking house builders in Britain were much influenced by the success of Bedford Park in London, which had received so much attention in the press that it was impossible not to know about it. Much of the journalism had mocked the 'pallid and pale, arty crafty' people who had moved in, but the arts and crafts were now fashionable, and there were plenty of young middle-class couples who thought that something like Bedford Park would be just the place for them and their Whistler etchings and willow-pattern plates. In Bristol, Sneyd Park was just that place, respectably far from the less exclusive areas on the other side of the Downs, near enough to the city centre to make easy the daily walk to work, and with the Downs and the Gorge to make it seem almost like living in the country. It had one other factor which raised it socially above the low life of the central city: it had no pubs, and the ground leases prohibited them for all time.

From the 1880s a number of estates were built in Sneyd Park, designed by the more recognisably arty – but respectable, of course – of the young architects in the city. The delightful Downs Park by Rodway and Dening springs to mind, but the best is probably Downleaze by Henry Dare Bryan. He started his practice in 1890 when he was 22, probably on the strength of this commission. Construction started in the following year and slowly worked westward as sales progressed, finishing eight years later. The houses are all large semi-detached pairs, and every pair is different. The north side, with houses mostly of stone to catch the sun, is the more conventional of the two, but very delightful. The south side, without much sun, relies on more colourful materials to enliven it. It is stunning. Not only is each pair different, each house in each pair is different. Despite this, the row forms a wonderfully cohesive group, its unity based on a limited range of colours running through all the houses, and a succession of gables of all possible sizes, stepping slowly down the sloping ground. The materials are stone rubble, used on the lower one or two storeys, with occasional red brick and much red tile-hanging above, and exposed timbering in some of the gables. All the external joinery is painted white. On both sides of the street there is also a small amount of Bath stone with a little shallow decorative carving here and there, fairly routine and not the work of an artist craftsman. When one examines the façades and the positions of the chimneys, it is clear that the basic plans of the houses are all much the same. Dare Bryan's prodigality of invention, which creates so much variety in a street of basically similar houses, is wonderful.

While all this was going on, he built another pair of houses, the White House and Grange Fell, in Leigh Woods (q.v.). At first sight they are so dissimilar to the houses in Downleaze that they could be the work of another architect, but when you examine them you see that the differences are in the colour of the materials, and that with more space at Leigh Woods Dare Bryan could stretch out the houses with two storeys instead of the three needed on the tighter Sneyd Park site. The same compositional skills are apparent in both.

Cabot Tower ⋆ Brandon Hill

1897

Brandon Hill was given to the Corporation in 1174, apart from an area at the top which belonged to the Abbots of Tewkesbury, who erected a chapel on it. After the Dissolution, the Corporation bought the Abbey's sequestered land and demolished the chapel. They have owned the whole of the hill ever since and we still have the ancient right to dry our clothes and beat our rugs on it.

In 1897, the four-hundredth anniversary of Cabot's discovery of Newfoundland, the Corporation decided to build a tower on the hill to celebrate his memory and beautify central Bristol by giving it a prominent landmark. The architect of the Cabot Tower was William Venn Gough.

Basically the tower is an exercise in Italian Gothic, but built of stone so familiarly local that the design's Italian derivation is not noticed – pink rubble sandstone banded with cream-coloured limestone. Near the top, each face of the tower has a highly romantic Romeo and Juliet balcony projecting from a Venetian Gothic arch, and at the very top there are spirelets and pinnacles clustered around a short spire crowned with an angel. Judged strictly as architecture it is really rather mediocre, but great fun and somehow lovable, perhaps owing to long familiarity. It is an essential part of Bristol's skyline and a reminder of the days when the Corporation would spend money on something entirely useless except to give people pleasure.

Former Fairfield School ★★

Fairfield Road, Montpelier

1898

Forster's famous Education Act of 1870 didn't make education compulsory, but it required the setting up of School Boards everywhere which could. The Bishop of Bath and Wells thundered against such wickedness – education made the lower classes dissatisfied with the station to which they had been allotted by God, and compulsory education was an infringement of the Englishman's liberties. Bristolians, more worried about an increase in their rates than a decrease in their liberties, agreed with him. Yet in the city at that time a third of all children were completely uneducated, never attending any school. They were the 'gutter children' of 'the vicious and dangerous classes'. The basic problem, which continued right through the nineteenth century and into the twentieth, was that although almost everybody agreed that teaching should be Christian, the Roman Catholics, the Anglicans and the dissenting churches, behind their polite smiles, hated each other. Though they only rarely said so explicitly, they would rather have no school than one which taught the un-Christian doctrine of a rival denomination. However, the Bristol School Board managed, very slowly, to transform education in Bristol, eventually building many schools and enlarging and improving others.

The models which most influenced school architects everywhere in England were those built by the London School Board. In Bristol most sites for new schools were large enough to allow buildings of no more than two storeys, so there were few of the towering structures which still dominate many districts in London. One of the exceptions was, and fortunately still is, the 1900 four-storey St George's School frowning down on Church Road in Redfield.

It is hard to select one from the many schools built in Bristol in the years up to and around 1900. Perhaps the most fascinating – though ugly fascinating – is Fairfield School in Montpelier, opened in 1898. Bits of it are single-storey, some two, most of it three and small parts, four. This variation is partly the result of the architect William Bernard's skilful use of the site's fall from side to side. His composition of the masses of the building, plus his profusion of towering gables and chimneys topped by a delightful little open-work cupola, is highly enjoyable.

But the colour! The mixture of red brick and grey and red sandstone may be to some people's taste – apparently it is – but it isn't to mine. The masonry is composed of large irregularly shaped uncut stones, fine in a barn but a doubtful choice for an urban building as large as this. In the upper part of the walls the stonework has been ruined by wide ribbon-pointing, presumably a later rain-proofing ordered by some aesthetically challenged official in the Education Department. It need not have been handled so brutally and could easily have been sympathetic. Despite all that, the building's picturesque massing makes this extraordinarily characterful building an unforgettable experience for the visitor, and a delightful and prominent feature on Bristol's skyline.

The school has now been re-located to new premises. The ground lease requires that the original building must serve an educational purpose, so its precise future use is uncertain.

Prudential Assurance Building ★★★★

17 Clare Street

1899-1901

Back in 1877 the Prudential Assurance Company had commissioned Alfred Waterhouse to design their headquarters in Holborn. He was then one of the most famous and successful architects in Britain. His efficiency, quite as much as the vast red terracotta palace he gave them, so delighted the company's directors that over the next decades they commissioned some 27 branch offices from him. Bristol's, built between 1899-1901, was the nineteenth. Like most of the other branches, it too was built of red terracotta.

Terracotta is a very hard, almost indestructible, fired clay which can be cheaply moulded into any shape or ornament required. It is not prone to staining, is rarely chipped or broken, and lasts almost for ever. Its good qualities are also its bad ones. Traditional building materials weather over time: the frost softens their sharp edges; the rain washes their exposed surfaces and allows dust and soot to gather in their protected ones, thus deepening their shadows; when the atmosphere is clean it allows lichens to mottle their surfaces. Terracotta allows none of those things. It doesn't weather, it remains forever sharp-edged, hard and unsympathetic. Having been widely popular ever since Waterhouse had used it on his Natural History Museum in 1870, by the late 1890s people had grown tired of it. The Bristol Pru was distinctly old-fashioned.

A building in the early-sixteenth-century style of François I, constructed in the early twentieth century in a material produced in a factory, was a matter of derision to the younger architects in Bristol, but a century later that is forgotten and we can enjoy it. We can also enjoy the riches of its ornaments up on the exposed and windswept roof, as we couldn't if they had been built of the softer Bath stone. The building has two street corners which Waterhouse celebrated by treating them as corner turrets with high conical roofs. They frame an elaborate gable which masses up with a high octagonal roof terminating in a magnificent chimney stack. This magical skyline is continued round the corner by a froth of gables on the Corn Street façade. Not the least of its pleasures is the green Cumberland slate roof, which contrasts beautifully with the red terracotta.

Probably the main reason for using red terracotta at Bristol was that it was indissolubly associated in the public mind with the Pru – an early example of branding. The seventy-year-old Waterhouse may not have kept up with fashion, but he never got into a rut. Every one of the 30-odd buildings he designed for the Company was individually crafted for its site and location. His Bristol branch is an enormous enrichment of the city's finest street.

Edward Everard's Printing Works ★★

Broad Street

1900-1

This printing works was designed by Henry Williams and built in 1900-1. In the early 1970s it was demolished to make way for redevelopment. Only this façade, and a short fragment of the building's red terracotta wall around the corner in John Street survive, and a single terracotta dragon of an original long row of them. The side wall was intended pop architecture which never became popular, ignored from the day it was completed to the day it was demolished. It was not really much of a loss. The façade, which is still with us, bore no more relation to it than it does today to the 1970s building which barges into its front so loutishly. Williams undoubtedly designed the bulk of the building, but who designed the façade? Tim Mowl was probably right in a sense when he said that the printer Everard himself was the most likely author. He was clearly proud of the art status that William Morris had conferred on his trade by taking up printing, and it must surely have been he who commissioned Doulton and Co. (detested by Morris!) to make his faience façade. The work was carried out by the recently appointed head of their architectural decoration department, W. J. Neatby, who must have been the actual designer, basing himself on Williams's plans. Gutenberg (mis-spelt!) and Morris work their presses on either side of the winged Spirit of Printing, under the supervision of Truth with her mirror and lamp. Everard undoubtedly thought this ceramic advertisement was high art. If the lately dead Morris had lived to see it he would have had one of his famous rages, as usual pulling out tufts of his beard, and if he had been able to read the description of the building in the government's 1994 List of Buildings of Special Architectural or Historic Interest, whose author also thought the façade was art – in the 'Pre-Raphaelite style'– he would have completed his depilation.

We, who have learned to enjoy popular, unsophisticated, art, can appreciate this façade designed as an advertising poster. But one is quite enough.

White House and Grange Fell ★★★★

Leigh Woods

1901

Semi-detached houses have been popular in England since the Regency period, though very rarely anywhere else. Occupying less land than detached houses and sharing a party wall, they are substantially cheaper than them but give an impression of greater size. By far the most common are those where the houses are identical. One of the most beautiful of this type is the pair at Buckingham Vale in Bristol (q.v.). But usually the most attractive are those, like this Leigh Woods pair, where each house is different but the two are designed to look like one.

White House and Grange Fell were built in 1901 to the design of Henry Dare Bryan, who a little later was to design his masterpiece, Western Congregational College

buildings because his windows usually had stone surrounds which he didn't want to hide. Dare Bryan's pair have no exposed stone, being entirely covered in white render, contrasting beautifully with the green shutters and window joinery. Dare Bryan made great play with his shutters, using them to elongate his windows so that they read almost as long strips. This horizontality is the core of the design, powerfully reinforced by the eaves, which continue across the gables on the right as a strip of lean-to roof. Because of these strong horizontal lines, the gables, dormer window, changing ridge line and chimneys are sufficiently controlled to contain the asymmetry. The balance is perfect.

(q.v.) opposite the Homeopathic Hospital. The obvious influence on these houses is Voysey, whose work was frequently illustrated in the architectural journals at that time, but the pair is in fact more original than first appears. Voysey never used external shutters on his

Scottish Provident Institution ★★★★

Clare Street

1902-3 Formerly Bristol Tramway and Carriage Company

The years of Edward VII's reign, almost the last of Britain's unrivalled national opulence, saw the peak of the nation's pride in its world empire, celebrated in literature by Kipling, in music by Elgar and in architecture by the neo-Baroque, the triumphalist style of Hope and Glory which suddenly became widely popular, producing a great crop of magnificent offices, hotels and town halls. In Bristol the Council had decided in 1897 that a new and much larger Council House was essential. If it had been built then it would no doubt have been Baroque, but unfortunately the councillors dithered for 38 years until 1935, when the Baroque had been replaced in popular esteem by the more sedate Neo-Georgian. So Bristol has only one, disappointing, municipal Baroque building, the Museum and Art Gallery, and two superlative small examples – the fountains outside the Victoria Rooms and this little office in Clare Street. It was designed by the partnership of Oatley and Lawrence and built in 1902-3.

The building is sited on the corner of Clare and St Stephen's Streets. Architects have always realised that one of the best ways of building on a corner is to design the building, or the front part of it, as a drum, so that both streets are fronted equally, and if necessary the main entrance can be positioned diagonally to open onto both. Few are as clever as this one, which is a square with its corners chamfered off, the entrance put into one of the chamfers, and the whole topped by a low circular dome. By sheer force of personality this little pavilion holds its own in a street of banks trying to shout each other down. Part of the piquancy of the design is the way the ground floor windows and doorway push up into the first floor, and the arched windows on the first floor push up into their steep pediments, quietly drawing attention to the shallow dome. Notice how satisfyingly the walls step back and forward, articulated by the coupled Ionic columns and their beautifully modeled entablature stepping backwards and forwards above them. Notice particularly how the crowning moulding of the cornice steps up to form the pediments. This is the design of a master.

The fine building we see today is very different from Oatley & Lawrence's original design for a larger, domed but essentially classical building. George White, the influential tramways and aircraft magnate, had offices opposite, at 28 Clare Street. He objected to the height of the proposed building. White wanted something that would complement his own offices, without overwhelming them. The Scottish Provident directors and their architect consulted with White throughout the design process, and the end result was this jewel-like little masterpiece.*

---

* I am indebted to Dr Sarah Whittingham's forthcoming biography of Sir George Oatley for the information about George White's involvement.

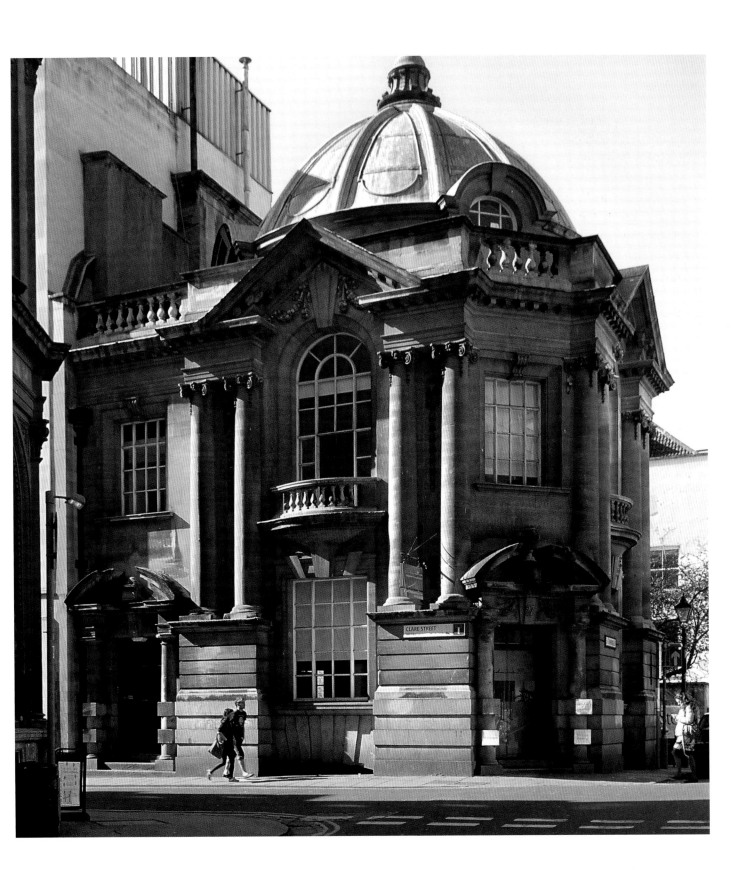

Bristol Museum and Art Gallery ★★

Queen's Road

1902-4

The top of Park Street contains two of the Wills family's numerous gifts to the city of their birth: the University tower and the City Museum and Art Gallery. One has only to look at the three huge red-brick bonded warehouses at Ashton – and remember that there used to be another, even bigger, on Canon's Marsh – to get some idea of the immense profits which came from cigarettes. When smoking was at its peak in the 1960s I remember being told, I don't know how truly, that every day at 3pm sharp, a man in a bowler hat carrying a rolled umbrella and a neat little briefcase, crossed Queen Square and went into the Customs and Excise office. He was delivering the daily cheque for over a million pounds excise duty.

The Museum and Art Gallery, originally only half its present size, was built between 1902 and 1904. The donor, Sir Henry William Wills, was not a modest man: he had his name and generosity recorded in letters a foot high on a huge plaque in the centre of the building's front. The building consisted of three storeys of galleries and offices built around a large glass-roofed court. The architect was Sir Henry's relative Frank Wills, working in association with a London firm of architects who doubtless did most of the work. The façade, presumably the design contribution of Mr Wills, is in a coarse version of the baroque which was then considered to be best suited to the land of Hope and Glory. It has the inevitable heavy rustication below, coupled Ionic columns above, a broken pediment and at the top three classical damsels representing painting, sculpture and architecture. Above the entrance and below Sir Henry's advertisement of his generosity, sits a curious little circular pavilion, completely out of scale with everything else, looking like one of the museum exhibits which has been put there temporarily and forgotten.

By the end of the First World War more galleries were needed, so Frank Wills, by

then Sir Frank, built an extension at the back, almost doubling the space, but again wasting most of it by arranging the accommodation around a huge roofed court. The money this time came from Sir George Alfred Wills.

Although I have included it in my Best 100, it is hard to say anything kind about this crude and boastful building, except that it houses some glorious things, and a bit of swagger in a street is always welcome on a grey morning.

Times and Mirror Building ★★★

St Stephen's Street

1902

The English Domestic Revival, an aspect of the Arts and Crafts movement, had a good, though late, innings in Bristol, producing houses, dock sheds, office buildings, a Congregational College, a huge nautical school (at Portishead) and this office for the *Times and Mirror*, Bristol's Conservative newspaper. It is in one of the narrow lanes which ran along the inside of the Norman city walls, this stretch now flattered by being called a street. It was built in 1902 and designed by Foster and Wood near the end of that practice's long and distinguished existence. Foster died at about that time and Wood was in his late seventies. The Times and Mirror Building is in a style not used previously by the practice, so it was almost certainly designed by Graham Awdry, who had joined the firm two or three years earlier and was soon to become a partner.

The factor which the architect had to remember here is that his building's façade, unlike that of most others, would never be seen from a distance. The carved name plaque, for example, is kept low because if it were any higher, as it normally would be to gain maximum publicity, it would never be seen. The ground floor is treated unmistakably as an office or printing works, its main window being a business-like grid of stone mullions and transoms. There would seem to be no particular reason why the upper floors should not have been equally business-like, but in fact they are thoroughly domestic in treatment. There was doubtless a psychological advantage to be gained in doing this: reporters and other staff would feel more comfortable in such a homely environment. (It is worth remembering that offices at that date had fireplaces and crackling fires in winter, and had to be small to keep warm. The impersonal open plan was far in the future.)

The upper three floors are lit by three large bay windows, treated differently on each floor but all having reassuringly ancient-looking mullions and leaded glass. The uppermost of these bays are linked together by a projecting strip of lean-to roof, making a very strong horizontal when one looks up at the façade, making plain that this is one building and not three. The result of all this is a thoroughly lovable building, very little known because of its tucked away, almost secret location.

20-24 Park Row ★★★
1902

These three houses built in 1902 by James Hart, an architect to whom no other buildings are attributed, demonstrate that he had great ability as a designer. According to Andrew Foyle the group was originally a decorator's showroom with a house on each side, which must mean that the shop-front of the house on the left is a later alteration. It is hard to be certain about the shop-front on the right, with its display window set back

moulded plasterwork around the oval windows and in the deep frieze displayed the opportunities he was offering his customers.

To the left of this ensemble is a row of four steeply gabled houses which were built three years later to the design of Edward Gabriel. Together with James Hart's three they make a splendid Arts and Crafts terrace.

behind a couple of Doric columns. This would have been an unusually expensive thing to do when the conversion from house to shop was made, and suggests that the columns and set-back are original.

The two outer houses, with their typically Arts and Crafts sloping buttresses (entirely useless structurally) and their oriel windows protected by overhanging gables, are charming but the decorator's house they frame, and to which they draw attention, is enchanting. Its first floor, with two oval windows flanking the central oriel, is thrust forward on brackets, shouting 'look at me'. It is a perfect piece of architectural advertising which must have delighted the decorator. The richly

Shirehampton Public Hall and Library ★★★★

Station Road

1904

In the years around 1900 there was an extraordinarily gifted group of young architects in Bristol, George Oatley, Henry Dare Bryan, Frederick Bligh Bond and several others. Bligh Bond, the designer of Shirehampton Public Hall, was a very fine architect, in my opinion probably at least as gifted as Sir George Oatley, but never given such marvellous opportunities. He was also an

to dig and what he would find there. Sure enough, when the workmen dug they found what Abbot Bere told them they would. Triumph! Bligh Bond was able to publish an entirely new account of the Abbey's architectural history. Alas! Later archaeologists found that Abbot Bere had lost his memory in the intervening 400 years, and was mistaken in much of what he dictated. Trenches

architectural historian and an early archaeologist, but unfortunately just one moulding short of the full entablature. In 1908, four years after he completed the Shirehampton Hall, he was appointed Director of Excavations at Glastonbury Abbey. Like so many naive souls drawn to Glastonbury he was fascinated by the legends and mystery of the place and soon came under the influence of spirits. To his distress he had no psychic powers of his own, but he teamed up with somebody who did and who was able to get in touch with the shades of long-dead monks. They communicated with him by directing his hand to write what they wanted to say. Bligh Bond, through his collaborator, asked them where

had to be filled in, new stonework removed and history re-written. Bligh Bond got the sack.

However, his dreamy gullibility didn't affect his skill at designing buildings of very high architectural quality, many of them in Shirehampton and the surrounding area. His Public Hall was completed in 1904 at a cost of £2,715 (including his fee of £68 10s). Most of his buildings are easily recognisable as his. He had absorbed some ideas from Norman Shaw and one or two other architects, but distilled them into a style of his own which was a continuation and development of the 1870s and '80s 'Queen Anne' domestic style. The main characteristics of his work are a fondness for white painted joinery; bow and dormer windows with exposed sash boxes; wide projecting eaves supported by timber modillions; and brick or stone walls with long and short stone quoins at the angles. This Hall is a typical example. (Not far away in the High Street, his beautiful house called The Wylands, is another, equally splendid.)

In the Public Hall the accommodation is arranged symmetrically about a large hall designed as an auditorium, with a sloping balcony at one end, still equipped with its original tip-up seating. The lesser rooms are in wings on either side of the entrance. This entrance could be a case study of Bligh Bond's method of design. The wide glazed doors are protected by a segmental hood arching over a sumptuous bull's-eye window giving extra daylight to the lobby. The hood is supported on beautifully carved wooden brackets with a richly modillioned cornice which continues over the windows on each side. They are flanked by the projecting wings which link the whole wide composition into a welcoming embrace. There is nothing pompous about any of this; it is thoroughly domestic in character.

The gable walls of the wings which face onto the street are another example. The sash windows at first-floor level are designed as a continuous strip which bulges out as a bow in the middle. Bow windows, often arranged in this way, are one of Bligh Bond's signatures. High above the entrance and the wings rises the huge roof of the auditorium. It is clad in the lovely grey-green Cumberland slates which were so popular at that time (partly perhaps because Wren, then the hero of the younger architects, had used them at Chelsea Hospital and Kensington Palace).

Like most of his contemporaries Bligh Bond had inherited a love of asymmetry from the Gothicists of a couple of generations back. The way in which he introduced it into this symmetrical building is another example of his cleverness. Part of his brief was to incorporate a public library. He put it to one side of the symmetrical part of his building and swept his great roof over it, dynamically projecting it forward at its peak. To mark the junction of Hall and library he placed a clock tower which is a little gem in itself. It is crowned by a very widely projecting modillioned cornice and a splendidly swirling double-curved baroque spire. Almost every other architect would have put the clock, more conveniently for maintenance, into the masonry tower, but Bligh Bond put it into the spire, with a little rectangular

bell louvre placed tight up under the cornice below.

The Hall stepped into history in 1920, when Vaughan Williams conducted the première of his *Lark Ascending* in it. It has been used continuously ever since, a focus for the communal life of an always vibrant community. Casual visitors to Shirehampton will probably miss it, tucked away inconspicuously in a road off the High Street. But it amply repays a visit, which must include a viewing of Bligh Bond's Wylands in the High Street, which now being in corporate ownership with more to spend on maintenance than the community association's Public Hall, is in sparkling condition, exactly as Bligh Bond left it. It is a tragedy that this brilliant man had so few opportunities. I am not aware of anything he built after the Public Hall was completed in 1904, though he presumably must have built something, since he lived until 1945. He wrote an excellent book on rood screens, a silly one on his experience at Glastonbury, and then faded out of history. Perhaps the stuffing was knocked out of him when he was sacked as Director of Excavations at Glastonbury Abbey. Presumably he became a joke. He died forgotten, whilst Sir George Oatley died five years later, full of honours and fame.

Wylands, Shirehampton

Cabot Café ★★★   38 College Green
1904 Currently vacant

The Art Nouveau period saw the first flowering of the tea shop, an institution which was to last until the coffee bar killed 'dainty teas' in the 1950s and '60s. Charles Rennie Mackintosh's tea rooms in Glasgow are now world-famous. The Cabot Café on College Green was never in their architectural class, but it was not too far below. It was designed by the Bristol architects LaTrobe and Weston and opened in 1904. The shopfront consisted of an entrance with elaborate Mackintoshian doors on the right and two large shop windows on the left. It's a pity it has been lost, but not a great tragedy because the façade above it was always a virtually self-contained entity and it survives intact, still sitting on a shopfront, though a different, routine one.

It is a beautiful and extremely clever design, well worth analysis. It consists of three vertical divisions, the two outer ones being treated as slim towers shooting upward with their arrowhead-like pediments. They frame the wider central bay which is more horizontal in its treatment, consisting of a two-storey bow window and a balcony bulging out between the towers. Note how neatly the semi-dome is contained within a wide sculpted arch. Now comes the really clever bit: if these three vertical elements were to make a satisfying unity they had to be tied together. This was done by setting them slightly forward from a wall at the top which stretches across the whole width of the façade, like someone standing behind three people and holding them within his outstretched arms. Below, the architects introduced a carefully controlled amount of colour into the façade by running a broad band of dark purple mosaic across the bow. This design is a masterly bravura performance for which one's admiration grows the more one studies it. But it is English bravura, not Continental.

It is instructive to compare this with what was happening at that time on the Continent – in Brussels, for example. There architectural imagination ran wild, discipline was thrown aside. Here in Bristol everything is controlled, understated and well behaved. In a term much used then but never now, it is a gentlemanly performance. A similar restraint occurred during the baroque period in England. Thomas Carlyle walked past Chelsea Hospital every day. After many years somebody told him it had been designed by Sir Christopher Wren. Carlyle said he had never really looked at it, but now he did he could see that it was the work of a gentleman.

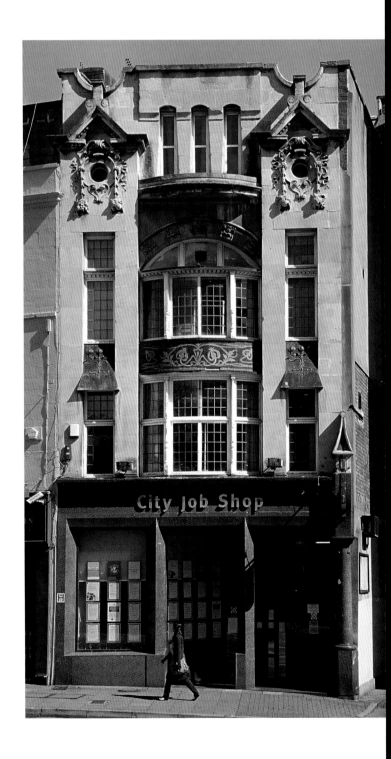

Western Congregational College ★★★★

Cotham Hill

1905-6 Now the Family (medical) Practice

In 1903 the Congregational Church held a competition for the design of a residential theological college to serve its western district, based in Bristol. It was won by the Bristol architect Henry Dare Bryan with a design in the then almost standard heavily rusticated Edwardian baroque. Shortly afterwards the church decided to make the college non-residential and asked Bryan to adapt his plan. Instead of tinkering with it, he sensibly went back to his drawing board and started again, this time coming up with the very different design we see today.

At that time the more progressive young architects in Britain were intrigued by a couple of houses which had been built on a sort of Y plan. The magazines had christened them butterfly plans because they consisted of a central block with wings going off at an angle of about 135°, and therefore looking a little like a butterfly. One of them had been built back in 1895, but the great Edwin Lutyens had completed one very recently. Bryan realised that if, on his corner site, he planned his College with two butterfly wings, he could adjust the angle so that his central block would face diagonally onto the road junction, and his southern wing would be at a right angle to

Cotham Hill, thus making its gable end parallel to the road. The result is that his building seems to fit onto its site naturally and inevitably, facing visitors as they come in from the gates on the corner, and throwing its arms open to welcome them. One feels that if the idea hadn't existed previously Bryan would have needed to invent it for this site.

Instead of his previous baroque, this time he chose an Arts and Crafts version of Jacobean, in other words a much lighter and playful version of real Jacobean heaviness. He used only a little carved ornament but he was wonderfully inventive in designing the profusion of towers, turrets, gables and finials. Inside, the accommodation is arranged around a Great Hall which rises through both storeys to a lantern in the roof. The first floor rooms are reached by a wooden balcony running round the Hall. At the back of the building is the delightful half-timbered Principal's House, facing onto Cotham Hill but set well back from it.

Bryan died in 1909, only a few years after the College was opened. He was just 41, a tragic loss to architecture in Bristol. His College is his finest work and one of the most enjoyable Arts and Crafts buildings in Bristol.

In the early 1990s the building was converted, with very little alteration, into a group medical practice, and given long overdue repairs.

Jamaica Street Carriage Works ★★★

1905, 1909

Now artists' and craftsmen's workshops

Throughout history there have always been vernacular buildings, i.e. those erected without the intervention of architects or other specialist designers. The term 'vernacular' is most frequently used of cottages, but applies equally to this carriage works. The development of iron, and later, steel construction, and the mass production of columns and beams, was shortly followed by the publication of tables of their various strengths (which had been ascertained empirically by engineers, no doubt with much extrapolation). Simple rules for calculating floor loads had long been known. The result was that small metal-framed buildings could be designed by anybody who could learn a few rules of thumb and do some simple sums. This encouraged the manufacturers of iron and steel structural components, and later the companies in every large town who erected them, to offer a free design service for the frame.

Metal-framed buildings could stand perfectly well without the support of heavy and expensive walls. All that was required was an envelope to keep out the weather and keep in the warmth, or at least some of it. If the appearance of the building was of no consequence, and for many industrialists it wasn't, no architect was required. In the Jamaica Street Carriage Works the outer envelope is no more than large windows between the columns. Originally of two storeys built in 1905, it was extended in 1909 by the addition of two further floors, this time with the columns sensibly cased in fire-protecting brickwork. It was extraordinarily old-fashioned, the frame being of cast-iron, long after it had been superceded by steel. (I wonder if the obsolete iron columns and beams were being sold off cheaply.) The ironwork was supplied and designed by J. L. Priest and Co., iron founders. Neither they, the builder, or the client would have considered the resulting building to be beautiful or an ornament to the street: they had simply achieved what they had set out to do: obtain the maximum amount of space for the least possible cost.

They didn't know that a few advanced architects in Europe, such as Victor Horta in Brussels, had produced somewhat similar glass-and-iron façades which *were* designed to be beautiful. Horta's did have some ornament, but within a couple of decades a growing number of other architects, pre-eminently Mies van der Rohe, were designing glass façades without it. Slowly, everybody's aesthetic boundaries were extended, so that most of us can now admire the Jamaica Street façade as its contemporaries could not. They would be bemused to learn that what they regarded as an abomination should be protected later in the century by the government, by listing it Grade II.

Tobacco Bonds ★★

A Bond, Cumberland Road, B Bond, Smeaton Road
C Bond, Clift House Road 1905, 1908, 1919
Now used for a variety of purposes

Nothing better illustrates the source of the Wills family's enormous wealth than these three huge warehouses, which held in bond their tobacco leaf before it was assessed for excise duty. Even these three were inadequate to cope with the vast amounts of tobacco imported by the company. In the 1920s a fourth bond had to be built on Canon's Marsh. Unlike the red-brick bonds it was a huge graceless concrete structure which never became popular. When the evil effects of smoking were finally acknowledged, sales of cigarettes throughout the world fell and the Canon's Marsh bond was the first to become redundant. One Sunday morning in 1988 huge crowds assembled on Brandon Hill to see it dynamited. As it dramatically collapsed into itself an immense cheer saluted its passing.

A Bond was built in 1905 with concrete floors carried on steel joists resting on concrete arches. B Bond of 1908 and C Bond of 1919 have structures entirely of reinforced concrete built on the Coignet system, for which Cowlins, their builder, held the licence.

The structural frames of all three are clad in brickwork, the ground storeys of Staffordshire blue engineering bricks, the upper eight of the local Cattybrook engineering bricks. The expensive Staffordshire blues have an extremely high compressive strength. This capacity was possibly needed on the lower part of the walls, but since they were carrying no loads other than their own weight it seems more probable that they were chosen for purely aesthetic reasons, to provide a dark base for the paler toned superstructure. The aesthetic problem with huge warehouses of this type is that they can seem to consist of nothing but hundreds of tiny identical windows. These tobacco bonds avoid that by having their long sides articulated by projecting bays in the centre and corner piers at the ends, and by string courses running right round them on every second floor. The buildings are capped by a high parapet hiding their roofs. Nobody could call the result beautiful, but the three huge buildings have a surprising dignity and poise, and over the years have come to be accepted as an essential part of Bristol's townscape and a fitting reminder of the long reign of tobacco and the Wills family. The man who designed them was the Wills company engineer, his identity otherwise unknown.

Central Library ★★★★★   College Green
1906

In 1902 the Corporation received a bequest of £50,000 to build a new library in place of the inadequate old one in King Street. The council decided to use the steeply sloping site on College Green, and hold a competition for the design. On the advice of the Royal Institute of British Architects, the architect E. W. Mountford was appointed to be the Assessor. He had himself won many competitions in the 22 years of his career to date, most recently the one for which he is best remembered today, the Old Bailey in London. One of his duties as the Assessor was to write the conditions for the competition. Since the library would have to abut the abbey's Norman and Tudor Gateway and stand immediately in front of the Gothic cathedral, it would have been usual at that time to require designs to be in a medieval style. Instead, clause 8 stated 'No special style of architecture is suggested, simplicity and breadth of effect are most desirable, the lavish use of ornament is to be avoided, and the cost of future maintenance should be borne in mind.' Today a condition like that would be unremarkable, indeed style would probably not be mentioned at all, but at that time, particularly for a site as sensitive as this one,

it was highly unusual. Apparently the freedom it offered encouraged a lot of architects to take part because 61 submissions were received. Mountford selected one sent in by H. Percy Adams, a well-known specialist in hospitals, but in fact designed by his 27-year-old assistant Charles Holden, working in his own time over two weeks in the evenings. The design was brilliant but utterly startling, like nothing seen before – and like nothing ever designed by Mountford himself. His Old Bailey, then under construction, was in the usual Edwardian baroque and all his previous work and all his subsequent buildings were in one or other of the classical styles. His acute perception in choosing something so foreign to his own work and to the way architecture seemed to be developing in England, was remarkable. So also was the decision of the Corporation to accept their Assessor's recommendation and instruct Percy Adams to go ahead with something many of them must have thought highly revolutionary.

Holden's competition drawings survive, somewhat tattered, in the RIBA Drawings Collection. They reveal that only minor changes were made to the elevations

when the Library was built. Those to the Deanery Road façade were slight proportional adjustments to some of its elements, no more. As this front has a different character to the back and sides, I will consider it first. Holden had to relate the Library and Gateway stylistically, and solve the problem caused by the necessity of making the Library higher than the Gateway. He resolved the height problem by setting back the upper storey of his Library so that the parapets of the Gateway and his first floor would line through. His parapet is somewhat false since the top floor is only two or three feet behind it and perfectly visible from Deanery Road. However, the stratagem works, the continuity of the strong horizontal

echoed the Gatehouse's Tudor mullions and transoms in all his windows and made a very complex play with variations of the tall bay window. Instead of single life-size statues in narrow niches on the narrow Gatehouse, he put groups of life-size figures in wide arched niches on the much wider central portion of his Library. The most subtle and satisfying link of all is the way the setting back and forward of flat surfaces seems to flicker over both façades. The result of this brilliant juxtaposition of two very different buildings is that each is enriched by the other: they have become one composition.

It is a great, though understandable, pity that this extraordinarily clever front has always been overshad-

provided by the two parapets makes an excellent link between the two buildings. There are many other links, the use of the same stone being the most obvious. (Mountford had sensibly insisted on its use in one of his conditions.) Another is Holden's shallowly projecting pavilions at both ends of his façade. Each is a simplified paraphrase of the Gatehouse, with a Norman-type arch on the ground floor and a tall oriel window above. He tied these end pavilions to his centre by using a simplified version of the arch in the three central bays. He

owed in critical estimation by the revolutionary back, beginning from the moment the 'Percy Adams' design was published in the architectural press, well before construction started. At the back and sides Holden felt less constrained by the past. Because of the fall in the ground the back is a full storey higher than the front, but appears even higher because Holden no longer needed to use the device he used on the front to make his façade seem as low as the Gateway. In the angle of the L-shaped side wall he placed a large staircase drum with its windows stepping down as the stair inside steps down. The lower group of these windows and the buttresses between them were one of the additions which Holden made to his competition design, thereby increasing its verticality. Around the corner the back elevation towers like a cliff. Here and on the side wall, Holden made another departure from his competition drawings by changing some of what had been ordinary windows into flat box-like oriels. Throughout these walls, the flatness of the surfaces, the jagged outline of the tower-like chimneys and buttresses, and everything's stark geometry without any softening of mouldings and ornament, were unprecedented in English architecture. Holden had leapt into the twentieth century.

At exactly the same time, Charles Rennie Mackintosh was making the same leap, at his School of Art in Glasgow. For the last 50 years scholars have been trying to work out who got there first and who influenced who. The debate is pointless. If one studies photographs of both buildings side by side it is apparent that there are no original details in either which are even roughly identical. What similarity there is, is in atmosphere: they employ a similar and strikingly new aesthetic which was also emerging on the Continent. The School of Art's first phase was built in 1897-9, and therefore pre-dates the Library. It contains nothing of a similar character to the Library except, perhaps, a certain harshness. The second phase, which is closer in atmosphere, was built in 1907-9, based on plans revised in 1906, so if there was a flow of influence from one architect to the other it came from Holden. Mackintosh's west façade is based on a succession of box-like oriels which are slightly similar to Holden's, but used in vertical strips which are quite unlike anything in the Library. However: history is littered with examples of scientists, mathematicians and artists making the same discoveries at the same time. The spirit of the age rules us all, but one or two remarkable individuals hear its call before everybody else, and occasionally two hear it at the same time. I think that is what happened here.

It has to be said that the exterior of Holden's Library, though ground-breaking and of very high quality, is greatly inferior to Mackintosh's. Its interiors are of only minor interest, whilst Mackintosh's are of superlative quality. Holden was a very good architect indeed: Mackintosh was a supremely great one. Holden lived into revered old age, having built an enormous number of buildings, some excellent, some less so. Mackintosh died forgotten and alcoholic, having built only a handful of buildings, but they are known and loved throughout the world.

In my opinion, Holden's Library, which was completed in 1906, is his finest building. In that year, still not a partner, he designed the new block of the Bristol Royal Infirmary. A splendid and historically important design, it was built in 1910-12, by which time the practice was at last called Adams and Holden. It has now been engulfed and ruined by the huge 1973 extensions.

St Alban's, Westbury Park ★★★★

Coldharbour Road

1907-9, 1913-15, 1920s

This fascinating church was the winning design in an architectural competition won by C. F. W. Dening in partnership with E. G. Rodway. Dening, its designer, had a distinguished background. He was articled to Henry Dare Bryan (architect of the Western Congregational College q.v.) and was then Holden's resident architect at the Library on College Green (q.v.) during its construction. He was 31 when work started at St Alban's.

It is odd that the congregation should have decided to build since it was only a few years since they had completed an earlier one. An exceedingly dull design by Crisp and Oatley, it was built in 1890 and now serves as the church hall. The new church was built in phases, first the nave and transepts from 1907-9, and then the chancel from 1913-15, but the last phase, which included a tower, was never built; the keyed stonework to receive it remains as a visible reminder that work is incomplete. I believe, although I am not quite certain, that the church is built of white lias, a stone which was quarried at Whitchurch and several places in Somerset. Whether it is lias or not, to most eyes it is an unattractive cheap material, too hard to be worked and therefore always used as rubble.

The exterior of the first phase, the nave and short transepts, is unremarkable, but the interior is notable for the unusual width of the nave, flooded with light from high clerestory windows. A most attractive and perhaps unique feature of the nave is that instead of having one great west window there are two, side by side. This was logical in such an exceptionally wide nave, but in a situation of that sort most architects would have had either one big one or three, to avoid the effect of splitting apart which two identical elements produce ('duality' in theoretical jargon). Dening, whose later writing reveals that he was thoroughly at home with classical theory, resolved the issue with aplomb by running the white strip of a balcony across the west wall, making a most ingenious and appealing composition of three elements. This and the great width of the nave were the first signs that he had greater depths than the rest of this otherwise uninteresting phase of work suggests.

The second phase, the east end of the church, displays something close to genius. It is hard to describe it

adequately in words or even in photographs because it is so complex. To comprehend it one must move about whilst looking all around one. Dening maintained the great height of the nave, but instead of its wide airy space made the east end into an inter-connecting complex of narrow soaring spaces. The change of character starts with the chancel arch, which is higher and narrower than the nave arcades. The side aisles continue eastwards as chapels, but in addition the chancel has very narrow, very high, aisles of its own. They are divided from the outer aisles and from the chancel by high columns which allow views through in every direction. This flow of space is obstructed on the north side by the organ, but

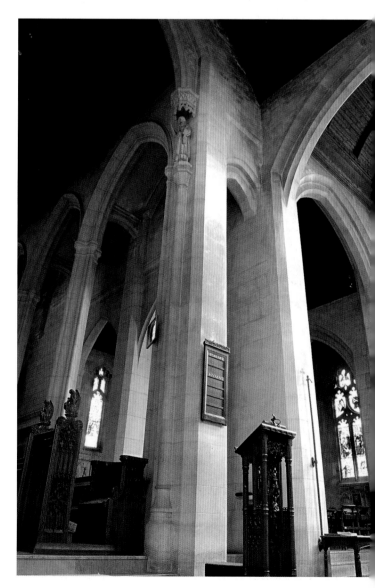

on the south side it is spectacular. I don't know whether these extraordinary chancel aisles had any functional justification, but their visual effect is stunning. No other church in Bristol has anything like it, and few have anything to rival it. An added pleasure at this end of the church's interior is that Dening was able to use only Bath stone, instead of the mixture of stones in the nave. Because the inner aisles go right up to the roof it was not possible for the chancel to have the clerestory windows that light the nave. They were not needed because the great east window admitted plenty of light, but ten years later this was severely limited when it was filled with stained glass. In consequence the chancel is now relatively dark.

The windows are one of the glories of St Alban's. A few in the north aisle are bog-standard, long-after-the-event, Victorian, but the rest are delightful Arts and Crafts work dating from the 1920s. They have none of the mawkish sentimentality of so much late Arts and Crafts work, nor any trace of modernism or Art Deco. They vary in quality: some, or perhaps most, are by the Bristolian Arnold Robinson, and the very best is his east window, a 1925 Great War memorial. It is superlative, perhaps the most beautiful painted glass of any period in Bristol. It alone makes a visit to this church a memorable and exciting event.

Externally the eastern end of the church is what everybody sees of it from the street: great stacks and crags of sheer wall; Gothic at its least archaeological but most dramatic and powerful. It owes a lot of its force to its craggy, hard, white stone. Whether Dening was forced to use it as an economy, or chose it because he knew he could use it expressively, he certainly made the most of it: a brilliant performance.

St Alban's was one of the last generation of Gothic churches: it shares the freedoms achieved by Dening's fellow architects of the Arts and Crafts movement, but it imitates nothing from them. It stands alone, one of the movement's triumphs and his finest building.

Clifton College Chapel ★★★★

College Road, Clifton

1909-10

Clifton College was one of the Victorian public schools founded to metamorphose middle-class boys into gentlemen through the infallible agency of cold baths and Gothic architecture. Since the College's Gothic buildings are somewhat mediocre one wonders what success they had. In 1907 the College authorities decided to enlarge their chapel, and naturally wanted to have a gentleman to design it. Fortunately one architect at the time was a baronet so they had no problem in making their choice: Sir Charles Nicholson.

The obvious thing to do was either to demolish the chapel altogether (which perhaps the authorities didn't want) or demolish one end and extend. Nicholson did neither, he retained both ends and demolished the middle, a quite extraordinary thing to do. He then filled the gap with a great hexagon of which the east and west sides connect to the remaining bits of the old nave. The result is very like the crossing in a cathedral, the east and west ends of the nave being equivalent to the transepts. The effect is stunning, but he had another firework to ignite. Above the hexagon he built the predictable hexagonal lantern, but less predictably, turned at an angle. (I suppose there is little doubt that his inspiration for all this was Ely Cathedral, of which the crossing is similar, but the idea of doing it in a little chapel was bold, to say the least.)

Unfortunately Nicholson's decorative gifts were not the equal of his spatial imagination. The Gothic windows in the lantern are conventional and dull. However they are high overhead and make little impact on this remarkable interior. It is engraved on the memories of thousands of Old Boys, but almost unknown to everybody else because it is seldom open to the public. Any chance to visit should not be missed.

There is one other distinguished building at the

College, the Memorial Gateway of about 1919, designed by Charles Holden, the architect of the BRI and the Library on College Green (q.v.). This can be seen by everybody because it is just off College Road.

The Royal West of England Academy ★★★★
Queen's Road, Clifton
1858, 1913

The Bristol Academy of painters, sculptors and architects was founded in 1844. In 1845 it received a gift of £2000 from Ellen Sharples, wife of a painter and mother of another, and on her death in 1849 she left a further £3400. These sums, then very large, decided the academicians to build their own premises. In 1852 they bought the site and the Bristol Society of Architects offered its members' professional services. Two architects submitted designs and the trustees decided to build to

As far as one can judge from old photographs, Hirst's façade was highly attractive, with the still existing five arches on the first floor then open as a loggia, and a huge monumental double flight of external steps leading up to it. It was a splendid, highly plastic composition, but not in the least user-friendly. By 1909 the academicians were forced to recognize that having to run up and down stairs in the rain was absurd, and that the loggia was a waste of valuable space, so the free services of the architectural profession were called upon again. Several architects were involved, but what we now see appears to have been largely the work of the not-very-well-known Bath architect, S.S. Reay. The resulting dull

Charles Underwood's plans and J. H. Hirst's elevations (a dreadful decision which must have been a nightmare for both of them). The building, with Underwood's superb top-lit galleries, and with uninspired façade sculptures by the over-prolific John Thomas (almost certainly the work of an assistant) was opened in 1858.*

façade was an unhappy mixture of Hirst's originally virile but now emasculated upper floor and attic, and Reay's routine Edwardian-French base. As far as the exterior is concerned the alterations were a disaster, but they produced two great internal benefits. The building works much better than it did before, and Reay's stair

*For information on John Thomas, see the entry on Lloyds Bank.

and entrance hall is a major triumph. The stair hall is planned on a generous scale and is entirely lined with sheets of white and grey marbles. The rather sombre but immensely dignified marble stair rises to a landing and then divides to ascend on each side up to the newly enclosed loggia. Above the stair is a dome, and in the lunettes lovely murals by Walter Crane. His colourful decorative style is the perfect foil to the cool marble below. This is one of the three or four finest classical interiors in Bristol; the whole building is superior to the rather leaden municipal museum and art gallery (q.v.).

Hirst's original façade [from *In Search of the Picturesque: the Early English Photographs of JWG Gutch*, Ian Sumner, Redcliffe/Westcliffe Books 2010], compared with today's

Wills Memorial Tower ★★★★★ Queen's Road
1914-25

The Wills family gave many buildings to Bristol: this tower and numerous other University buildings, the Museum and Art Gallery, the Homoeopathic Hospital, St Monica Home of Rest and many others. In addition they built plentifully for themselves: their factories in Bedminster, their bonded warehouses, and family homes in and around the City. Bristol is almost unthinkable without them.

Two brothers, Sir George and Henry Wills, paid for the University tower, and selected their fellow Congregationalist, George Oatley, as their architect. Their stated purpose was to give the University a physical prominence which until then it had lacked, and the city of their birth an ornament. Sir George asked Oatley for classical and Gothic alternative designs. It would have been obvious to Oatley that no classical tower could ever have the size and dominance at the top of Park Street that a Gothic one could have, and presumably he explained this to the brothers. He produced his design in 1912 and work began in 1914. It was interrupted by the war, recommenced in 1919 and completed in 1925.

Oatley was an unusual man. The dominant force in his life was his religion, and the fact that when, at the age of nine, he had lost both his parents, he and his four siblings were taken in by an aunt with very little money. When he became successful he in turn supported several poor families in Bristol, never, despite his huge fee income, becoming rich. When he died he left a mere £12,000. He believed that any talent he might possess was given to him by God, and that any praise was due to God and not to him. He never welcomed publicity or sought to advance himself. He was prepared to design buildings in almost any style if his client wanted it, though his love of Georgian architecture may suggest that he was happiest designing classical buildings. This is probably confirmed by the fact that his best building apart from the tower is the enchanting baroque jewel he built for the Scottish Provident Institution in Clare Street (q.v.). However, many of his works are hard to admire, and a few, like the University's horrible Physics Building, are downright ugly. Others, like Wills Hall on the Downs, which is a grossly inflated Cotswold manor house, or West India House facing Bristol Bridge, are simply boring. So what of the University tower?

It is, beyond any question, a resounding success, a triumphant achievement of what Oatley had been asked to do – to give the University and the city something which would be an outstanding ornament to both. Either he, or more probably the Wills brothers, decided that the best way to do this was to build a tower tall enough to appear in views across the City. Oatley decided that to make his tower tell to maximum effect in these long views, it would have to be not only tall but massive, and its main elements big. His success in doing that can be best appreciated in the view which must have been uppermost in his mind, the one looking up Park Street. The tower inevitably faces onto Queen's Road, which meant that it would be seen obliquely from Park Street. It is from there that the massiveness of the tower and its elements is most apparent. The great windows are so huge that the Georgian houses which march up the hill towards them, could, if they continued, march right through them, losing only their chimney stacks on the way. This massiveness can produce startling results in some of the nearer views, such as the one from the uphill side of Berkeley Square. In some lights it is surreal because the discrepancy of scale between the intervening houses and the tower is so great that the tower seems closer than the houses.

In a classical building such giantism can be brutal, but with Gothic there is always plenty of small scale ornament to clothe and humanise it. The supports of the tower, both visually and structurally, are the huge corner piers which rise up to the pinnacles with only the slightest diminution, but they are made to seem slender by the recessed panelling which shoots up the middle of each of their faces. The huge windows are deeply recessed back from the face of the piers, making their structural function perfectly clear – if the windows were removed the tower would still stand securely on its four great legs. At the top the tower breaks into a froth of pinnacles, panels and crockets from which the huge octagonal lantern emerges, clasped by the stubby little spires surmounting the piers. When some of the larger medieval Gothic churches are seen from a distance their ornaments fail to make much impact because they are too small. They rely on the larger masses and their silhouette. Oatley's ability to get the scale of the ornament on his

tower exactly right for distant as well as close-up views is almost uncanny. The tower's simple silhouette, its contrast between areas of plain wall and froth, and above all, its huge size, are extraordinarily moving. It is a wonderful civic ornament.

The interior is no disappointment; indeed it is a stunning experience to see it for the first time or after a long interval. One enters into a cathedral-like hall with a fan vault lost high above one's head. Before one, rising slowly up to a gallery at the rear, are two great ceremonial stairs, one on each side. How many people, feasting on this glorious interior, realise that the tower is that rare and wonderful thing, an almost entirely useless object placed here purely to give pleasure. But pleasure, of course, is not useless. It is impossible to envisage Bristol without Oatley's tower.

Whiteladies Cinema ★★ Whiteladies Road

1911

Now partly a restaurant; otherwise awaiting redevelopment

History will probably decide that movies were the defining art form of the twentieth century and cinemas one of its most characteristic building types. It is hard now to recognise how universal cinemas used to be; over the years Bristol had 61 of them. Today, apart from a few sad and mutilated fronts, they have all gone, replaced by television and the multiplexes. The earliest permanent picture house in Bristol, the Bio, was converted from the old Counterslip Hall in 1908. The first purpose-built cinema, the Queen's Hall in Peter Street, was opened in 1910. The Whiteladies Picture House was the first 'cinema group' in Bristol, an entertainment complex with, in this case, a restaurant opening off the foyer and an upstairs dance hall with a sprung floor. It opened in 1921 and was designed by the architects LaTrobe and Weston.

The interior, of only minor architectural interest, has suffered from alterations, but the much more interesting Art Deco exterior survives almost intact, though now tatty and peeling. On the street frontage, beside the restaurant and jammed in front of what used to be a grim Victorian nunnery, is a tiny porch with Ionic columns and mosaic floor. Rising on the corner just behind is the splendid tower, square below and octagonal above, with name panels linking square and octagon on four sides and pierced stone grilles alternating on the others. It is topped by a tiny dome and is all intact and original. The long side wall on Melrose Place is hard to fathom because of a subsequent alteration. One feature has always delighted me, the sequence of three pairs of windows or ventilation grilles at the far end, high up on the wall, with wonderful winged features supporting them and then dropping down as pendants.

The tower is built of Bath stone, the side wall is rendered and probably always has been. The architect Tom Burrough, who had known the cinema since it was built, wrote in 1970 that the whole exterior was painted white. I think he was mistaken about the tower: I cannot believe the architects would have allowed their beautiful Bath stone to have been painted. I wonder whether, if the budget had been greater, they would have wanted their winged features to be picked out in colour. Seventeen years earlier they had designed the Cabot Café on College Green (q.v.), which has delicious touches of colour. What was appropriate for the café's Art Nouveau was even more appropriate for the cinema's Art Deco.

We must all hope that some profitable use will be found for the building, and that the exterior at least will be sensitively restored. It is shocking, though not surprising, that it was not protected by being listed until 1999. By sheer good luck the exterior of what was probably Bristol's architecturally best cinema survives almost intact. It has been empty and neglected for far too long.

Concrete House ★★★★★

4, The Ridgeway, Westbury-on-Trym

1934-5

This highly important house was built in 1934-5, to the design of Amyas Connell and Basil Ward. Most of their work was done a little later when they were joined by a third partner and became famous – or notorious to many people – as Connell, Ward and Lucas.

Concrete House was the first in Britain to be designed on the lines of Le Corbusier's Domino houses, in which the concrete floors and roof slabs were supported on columns which could be placed wherever convenient. This gave unheard-of freedom to architects, who could put rooms and walls wherever they wanted, without having to worry about the need to plan walls over walls on the floor below. Le Corbusier's brilliantly seductive perspective diagram kept even the stair outside his rectangular slabs in order to demonstrate this. But as the wonderful houses he built on this system demonstrated, slabs did not have to be rectangular, nor did they have to be all the same shape on successive floors. The architect was free to enclose his building with either wall or glass as the use of the room dictated and his sense of design determined. At that period all Le Corbusier's external walls were white concrete, and so powerful was the magnetism of his work that his followers followed suit. (His genius as a designer was almost equalled by his genius as a publicist. An example of this is his decision to use an intriguing pseudonym instead of the more pedestrian Charles-Éduard Jeanneret.)

At Concrete House the concrete columns are spaced 12 feet apart in one direction and 14ft 9in or 8ft 2in in the other. It was important to demonstrate the simplicity of the structural idea, so the floor slab projects over the living room and one of the bedroom windows, and the stair, following Le Corbusier's diagram, projects from the house in a glass box. The ideas were not original, but the way the separate elements were put together was, and this little jewel, after loving restoration, looks as exciting and brave as it must have done when new.

Unfortunately, a great deal of restoration was needed. When I first trespassed into the garden in the early 1950s or thereabouts, it looked almost ready for demolition. The problem was that in the past builders and architects never needed to worry about insulation or condensation because the thickness of walls and roofs gave adequate heat insulation as an almost unregarded by-product. Building science wasn't needed, so architects understood very little about it. The thin concrete walls and slabs of all these early modern houses in cold and rainy Britain had very little insulation value, causing devastating condensation; and the metal windows, before the introduction of hot-dip galvanising, corroded terribly.

Fortunately, modern technology and knowledge have made it possible to correct all these faults, though at very great expense. The 1930s was the heroic age of modern architecture in Britain; perhaps, with hindsight, more heroic for owners than architects.

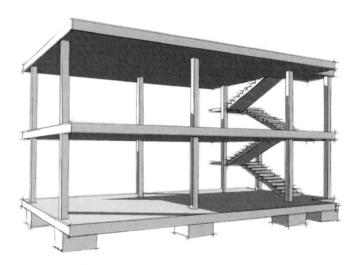

Le Corbusier's diagram of a Domino house structure

The Council House ★ College Green
1935-52

Bristol has always called its town hall the Council House. The present one is the fourth. In 1897 the Council realised that their 1824 one (q.v.) was too small and a new one on a new site was essential. Sixteen years later they started to buy options on the houses on the west side of College Green, and sixteen years after that decided to hold a competition for a new building. Sir George Oatley's partner G.C. Lawrence and a London specialist in town halls, E. Vincent Harris, were appointed to act as assessors. Harris dismissed all the entries as useless and manoeuvered himself into the job. Lawrence resigned in disgust, architects in Bristol seethed, and the Royal Institute of British Architects reprimanded Harris. But he had the job and sailed on regardless, designing the building we see today. Work started in 1935, was interrupted by the war, and was finally completed in 1952, fifty five years after it had been decided to build it.

Some of the better Harris buildings are pleasant pastiches of the great Edwin Lutyens's work, for example the County Hall at Taunton which he finished in 1932, just before he started to design the Bristol building. Never a man to waste a good idea he used the same details at Bristol. But here it wasn't a good idea because the Council House is vastly bigger than the County Hall, and its façade of Lutyens windows and brickwork, which looks fine there, is stretched from Deanery Road all the way to Park Street. This great length of boredom is relieved to some extent by the end pavilions and the delightful domed temple in the middle – delightful because it's an outrageous crib from Lutyens. However, there is one feature which is entirely original, the huge lead roof. Harris should have stuck with Lutyens, who was good at roofs, because it is the roof which kills the Council House. To be fair, he always intended that it would be crowned by an ornate lead cresting which had to be omitted because of its cost, but I can't see how that would have helped much.

There are, however, some good things about the building. The great Imperial colonnades at the back and the Augustan steps going down to them from Park Street, are magnificent and original. When he took the trouble he could design well. Some of the committee rooms are glorious and Cowlin's craftsmanship, inside and out, is superb: Harris certainly knew how to run a contract. But the building's essential absurdity and lack of principle is revealed in the only two windows singled out for special treatment, those on the first floor of the high end-pavilions. Each of them, with its stone columns and balcony, would have cost as much as a council house. People looking up at them must think they light the offices of great nobs, perhaps the Lord Mayor and the High Sheriff, and are designed so that they can address multitudes from the balconies. But no, when you look carefully you can see through the windows a row of WC cisterns: they are the toilets. There isn't even any access to the balconies. That sort of useless extravagance is almost criminal. No decent architect, and certainly not Lutyens, would have done such a thing.

When I was a student I absorbed the Bristol architects' contempt for the way Harris had elbowed himself into the job. I am probably prejudiced against him still. But I have had many years to look at the Council House and to think about it. I can enjoy bits, but I cannot love the whole. Next time you pass, have a close look at the brickwork with its specially made long thin Roman bricks and their wide joints. You will never see better craftsmanship. Cowlins came out of this sorry tale triumphantly; Harris with his reputation in tatters.

Electricity House ★★★   Colston Avenue
1938-40 Now Royal Sun Alliance

This building has never had the appreciation I think it deserves. The best that anyone has said about it is that it was the first building in Bristol to have an underground car park. It has qualities much more important than that. It was designed by Sir Giles Gilbert Scott (designer of the superb Anglican Liverpool Cathedral) and built in 1938 to house the offices and showrooms of what was later to be known as the South Western Electricity Board. In 1940, just before its final completion, it was requisitioned by the Air Ministry and not properly

finished until it was released in 1948. Even then, government-imposed financial stringency prevented the removal of an extremely ugly mortar slurry which had been applied to protect the stonework during construction. It so obscured the building's attraction that few people at that time could appreciate its quality. I remember how my eyes were opened, decades later, when the stonework was at last cleaned.

The long narrow site, facing into the Centre and squeezed between two roads, more or less determined the building's form. Its facing material, Portland stone, has been much criticised as being unsuitable for a town of red brick and Bath stone. Scott's obvious reason for choosing it, apart from love of the material, is its far greater resistance to decay than Bath stone. As things have turned out, the choice was successful in every way, since there are now few Bath stone buildings in the vicinity and many reinforced concrete ones: in that motley company the white stone shines out.

In the years around 1900 when Scott began practice, there was much debate about how to design a heavy-looking building when it had to have a row of showroom windows. Architects were accustomed to treat ground floors as strong bases visually supporting the floors above, and found it offensive to see buildings apparently supported on sheets of glass. In the 1920s Le Corbusier showed that a building appearing to float above ground without visible support could be exciting and attractive (and logical when, as at Electricity House, the building depended for its support on slender steel or concrete columns and not on its walls), but at that time few English architects could accept that. For his Electricity House Scott designed an alternative, more academic, solution. He set the glass of his showroom windows well back from the piers between them, so that the building appears to sit on a long row of sturdy piers. My admiration for Le Corbusier is unfashionably high, but I think Scott's solution is equally valid and attractive. The building's dynamic form, surging towards the City Centre, depends on the horizontal lines of these piers and their capping, and on the recessed top floor and projecting roof slab. Scott modified this forward surge by projecting the side walls at the point where the curve of the prow meets the flat sides.

This is a building I have grown to appreciate. When I was young we despised it because it was insufficiently 'modern'. Next time you are in the area, compare this work of a very fine architect, with a remarkably similar building in Broadmead by a decent but lesser architect – the store now occupied by Primark. It's a perfectly pleasant building, but every one of its features is inferior to Scott's equivalent.

There is a second, delightful, Scott building in Bristol, 37 and 39 Corn Street (below). Scott was commissioned to uplift the design of a commercial architect. Again he used Portland stone, justifiably in this street of huge variety. The building is enhanced by the decorative sculpture of Hermon Cawthra.

The Robinson Building   Redcliffe Street
1963

E. S. & A. Robinson began in 1844 when Elisha Smith Robinson started selling wrapping paper to grocers. His personality soon made him a leading figure in Victorian Bristol, and his business genius created a very large company engaged in all aspects of packaging. In 1876 he built the works and offices which after war damage were demolished in 1960 to make way for the present building. In the years after 1945 the company continued to grow vigorously, with subsidiary companies, factories and offices throughout the country. At the end of the 1940s it set up its own architects' department, which under its chief architect, John Collins, established a national reputation for the quality of its design. In the 1980s the company lost its separate identity in a series of take-overs.

The 15-storey building, which was completed in 1963, was the first tower block in Bristol and remains one of the best. It is square on plan, standing on tall piers with the glazing of the reception area set well back behind them, giving the building a firm visual base. Above this, it consists of a grid of concrete columns and wall panels faced with white Carrara marble aggregate. The windows are set deeply into their reveals, giving the faces of the building an attractively shadowed and solid appearance, instead of the smooth flat walls of most office blocks. Above is a high parapet, making a satisfactory capping. Originally the windows, and therefore the grid, were designed to be rectangular, but when the drawings were about to be submitted to the company's Board for approval, Collins felt that it was too bleak and the entire project might be dropped. It was then suggested that if the tops of the windows were arched, in a paraphrase of Bristol's Victorian buildings (and particularly of Elisha Smith Robinson's arched building) the project would be more likely to be approved, and the arch idea could be reconsidered later. The Board approved and particularly commended the arches. So reconsideration was no more than a process of refining.

Buildings of the 1960s are now at the bottom of the inevitable revolution of taste. Nobody loves them. They are as despised as Victorian buildings used to be in 1963 when Elisha Smith Robinson's handsome building was demolished. There are signs that the equally inevitable return to favour is starting. Already a few 1960s buildings in London have been listed. It won't be long before some in Bristol will follow: it's a fair bet that one of the first will be the Robinson Building. Until then it is at risk from developers and ignorant planners.

Pitch and Pay Pitch and Pay Lane, Sneyd Park
1963-5

In the decades after 1945 the design of speculative housing was at a particularly low ebb. Most housing estates were no more than rows of brick semis, varied by as many different coloured bricks and roofing tiles as the builder could obtain. In order to cram in as many houses as possible, existing features such as ponds, trees, hedges

and walls were usually destroyed. Housing was scarce so it was a sellers' market, with house builders believing that since everything they built was sold, people wanted nothing different. They also knew that if they built something which people did not want, they would quickly become bankrupt, so experimentation was rare. Architects, knowing that their hands would be tied by the developers, were reluctant to become involved.

This changed dramatically with the arrival of Span Developments. The company was founded in the mid-1950s by two idealistic architects, the highly gifted designer Eric Lyons and the businessman G. P. Townsend. Because architects were forbidden by their professional Institute from taking any part in contracting or developing, Townsend resigned his membership and became a developer, using Lyons as his architect. Span estates had several things in common: they were quite small; the management of each estate after completion was vested in a committee of its owners;

existing features were preserved and often provided the stimulus for the layout; they were landscaped to an unprecedentally high standard; houses had pitched roofs and were constructed of well-tried materials and techniques; and the design was uniformly excellent, but different from estate to estate. The houses weren't cheap, selling mainly to professional and business people, but the estates were such an enormous success and attracted so much publicity that housing developers couldn't ignore them. Many did their best to jump on the bandwagon, selecting a few of the Span ideas and applying them to cheaper mass housing. The results were variable, but there was a distinct improvement in the quality of housing in this country. As a result many architects who had previously spurned spec. housing changed their attitude. It is not an exaggeration to say that Lyons and Townsend caused a revolution.

Occasionally when Span bought sites outside London they employed respected local architects to design them. Pitch and Pay is an example. It was designed by Michael Hitchings, at that time a partner in Towning Hill and Partners, and built in 1963-5. The layout is delightful, and the design of the houses is ingenious and highly attractive. Everything at ground floor level, including the garages, is built of dark coloured bricks. Everything above is white. The first floors project a metre or so from the dark walling below them, so that they seem to float – the antithesis of the spec. builder's earthbound brick box. Basically the houses are traditional, but with a character that was entirely new. The landscaping, by Span's Prebend Jakobsen, is as always, excellent, depending on a few old walls, some large mature trees and much new planting, now itself mature.

The Colston Tower   Colston Avenue

1970-72

This 18-storey tower was designed by my practice Moxley, Jenner and Partners and built in 1970-72. One of the determining factors in the design of tall office buildings is the obvious need to get adequate daylighting to the back of the offices. It is therefore logical to have continuous windows. Another less obvious factor is the need to protect against the risk of a fire on one floor spreading through the heat-shattered windows into the floor above. The usual protection against this is to have a spandrel wall up to cill height, separating the glass on each floor. This tends to mean that office blocks all look much the same as each other. My partner Michael Hitchings suggested an ingenious variation: instead of having a separating spandrel wall, why not make it horizontal instead of vertical, by projecting the floor slab by an equivalent distance. This has several additional advantages: its shadowing reduces solar heat gain; it provides escape routes in case of fire (additional to those inside the building); it provides maintenance ways for window cleaning and repairs; and it gives protection to office workers against sensations of vertigo. It even reduced the cost of scaffolding.

At the base of the tower there is a long, vertically louvred, horizontal wing. In order to retain it as a separate element contrasting with the verticality of the Tower, the floor of the podium below it is deeply recessed, so that it seems to float above it. In the late 1960s and early '70s when the Tower was built, the city planners determined to have a series of elevated walkways crossing the Centre. They were to be built piecemeal as buildings around the Centre were rebuilt, which they felt sure was inevitable. In fact, very few were rebuilt, so a few years later when the planners passed to their next enthusiasm, the plan was dropped. Unfortunately we and our clients had been obliged to build a now entirely useless walkway on the south side of the podium and the stub of one of the bridges planned to cross the Centre. Many people must have been puzzled by the confusion at this point in the design.

Clifton Cathedral   Pembroke Road
1973

In 1834 the Roman Catholic Church started to build a large classical Pro-cathedral in Triangle West, ready for the day when English bishops would again be appointed by the Vatican and it could become a real cathedral. It was far too ambitious and was never finished. In 1846 an Italian Romanesque church with an extraordinarily dismal interior was built on its stump. Finally, a century and a quarter later, the Church decided to abandon the old building and start again on a new site. The old building remained unused, ugly and decaying, preserved on an extremely valuable site only because nobody could suggest a new economic use for it, or had the courage to allow it to be demolished. It is at last (2010) being redeveloped.

In 1850, to intense fury in England, Pope Pius IX had

All the interior surfaces apart from the pale marble floor are a lovely cool greyish-white concrete, left rough from the wooden shutters in which they were cast, but built with consummate care and attention to detail. Visitors enter a low-ceilinged narthex lit by the only windows in the building, both filled with very beautiful non-figurative coloured glass. After a few steps visitors leave this confined space and enter the huge volume of the nave. The sense of release is palpable. Daylight floods down from a huge lantern hidden high overhead. It is supported on three sides by a wall and on three by a huge concrete ring-beam pierced by great hexagonal holes to lighten its weight both physically and visually. The complicated concrete roof structure is further complicated by wooden acoustic cones. Beneath all this intricacy there is something remarkably moving in the simplicity of the great concrete wall which forms the

reintroduced Catholic sees into Britain, and to avoid confusion the Bristol diocese was named Clifton. The new Cathedral, dedicated to SS Peter and Paul, is in Pembroke Road and was completed in 1973, designed by the Percy Thomas Partnership to meet the liturgical requirements introduced by the Second Vatican Council. Accordingly the altar is brought forward and the congregation is seated on three sides around it. The centrality of the altar determined the entire design. Unlike Liverpool's Roman Catholic Cathedral, which is circular, Clifton's is an elongated hexagon, making possible a more complex and subtle interior than Liverpool's, where everything can be comprehended at a glance.

back three sides of the hexagon, folding round the altar and the Bishop's throne.

The coloured glass is by Henry Haig, the delightful font set in a pool of water is by Simon Verity, and the altar and lectern were designed by Ronald Weeks. The Stations of the Cross were cast and cut into the concrete walls by William Mitchell. Their expressionist imagery seems crude to me, but their collective effect is the exact opposite. Being the same material and colour as the walls of which they are part, they fit into the interior quietly, almost inevitably. Like the main body of the church, they are lit from hidden skylights.

Unfortunately I find the exterior extremely ugly. To some extent that is due to huge areas of concrete having gone black, but even when that is corrected (as it could be) all the forms seem lumpish, with none of the complexity and subtlety of the interior. In the tower the huge areas of blank walling, despite being faced with pinkish brown granite chippings (the colour of much local stonework) seem foreign in these streets of highly elaborated Victorian houses. The Cathedral appears to be trying, but failing dreadfully, to fit in. The triple concrete spire is more successful, but would have been more so if it were higher. That was prevented by the city planners, who stupidly decreed that it should not rival the spire of Christ Church on Clifton Green.

It is the inside which matters most. For me, it is one of the great interiors of the last 50 years in Britain.

High Kingsdown
1975

In the early 1950s Kingsdown was an area of eighteenth- and nineteenth-century artisan cottages and tradesmen's terrace houses. It was an enchantment, never to be forgotten by those who knew it: a hillside suburb hanging over the city below. There was nothing like it, anywhere. But it had a lethal disability: property values were low, most of the houses were in poor condition and many were derelict. To eyes blind to enchantment, it was ripe for redevelopment. The Infirmary snatched part of the slopes and the Council took the rest for 'slum clearance', building high blocks of flats at right angles to the slopes. Local activists, increasingly aware of the value of what had been lost and detesting what was replacing it, were outraged. Battle was finally joined over an area at the top – High Kingsdown. The City Architect, Albert Clarke, almost certainly more sensitive to the situation than his position allowed him to say, prepared a very decent scheme of low-density council housing, but the Government rejected it because the density was much too low. So he had no option but to design a scheme of 16-storey flats, later, after much agitation, reduced to 14. The uproar increased and reached the national media. Finally the Council, by then Conservative, reversed the policy and appointed an outside firm of architects to design a low-rise, high-density scheme, this time of private houses and flats.

The architects chosen were Whicheloe and Macfarlane, who produced the scheme approximately as it exists today. The City then invited builders to submit offers for the land and the scheme attached to it, and JT Building Group's bid was accepted. The Group had its own architects'department, under the leadership of Roger Mortimer. They developed the plans and house designs but maintained the purity of the concept – inspired by a little development in Denmark by the great Jørn Utzon (of Sydney Opera House fame). Building was completed in 1975.

The two-storey houses are L-shaped on plan, with all the main windows facing south or west onto small garden courts made private by the high walls of the adjoining houses. The 100 houses are arranged in echelon, in blocks reached by a network of pedestrian footpaths threading between them, and made magical by plants hanging over the high garden walls. Garages

and parking spaces are kept to the periphery of the site.
One of the great pleasures of the scheme is the rough-
textured tawny brickwork, and the way that all the walls
are topped by pantiles, giving them a delightful curly
capping. Pantiles, Bristol's traditional roofing material,
are also used on the roofs. Most houses have three
bedrooms, some have a fourth achieved by adding it onto
the end of the house by bridging it over the adjoining
footpath. High Kingsdown is that rare thing in Bristol, a
development as enjoyable as the environment it replaced.

When it was planned it was the council's intention to
smash the Inner Ring Road through Kingsdown and
Cotham, along the line of Cotham Road. In order to
protect the houses from the consequent noise and pollu-
tion, the architects built a protective wall of flats, with
its main rooms facing south, away from the road, which,
mercifully, was never built.

Bank House   Sheepway, Portbury

1991

This large and outstandingly beautiful house is one of greater Bristol's secret treasures, being completely invisible from outside its own site. It was built by the architect Michael Axford for himself and his wife in 1991. His basic concept was a cloister, where all the rooms look inward onto a court, which in this case is a swimming pool. There are only a few small windows in the outer walls, some positioned to allow specific views. The large amount of top and sub-soil which had to be removed before building could begin was piled around the perimeter of the site to form a 2m to 3m bank heavily planted with trees and shrubs, now approaching maturity. This gives total privacy within the site and a pleasant appearance for neighbours and passers-by on the road. A partial gap in the planting is carefully positioned to frame a view south over a wooded valley, whilst still preserving privacy within.

The house is built on the western half of the nearly square site, the eastern half being occupied by a tennis court. Visitors enter at the extreme eastern corner so that there is a wooded drive winding up to the house, which only becomes visible at the end. They enter a long picture gallery leading to an octagonal hall. Only after leaving that do they see the pool and the panorama of rooms around it, all faced with walls of glass. The arrangement of the rooms around the pool was dictated by the movement of the sun so that the master bedroom receives its first rays, the kitchen in the centre gets the longest exposure and the sitting room faces the sunset.

The house is warmed by under-floor heating arranged in 16 zones, computer-controlled to respond to solar heat gain, and the level of insulation is high. Walls, floors, ceilings and furnishings are all white. Throughout the house the degree of control, down to the smallest detail, is extraordinary. Taps, work surfaces, cupboards, door knobs, picture hanging – everything – is designed and considered with absolute precision.

In a single-storey house of this size a large amount of

RAC Supercentre Great Park Road, Bradley Stoke
1993-5

This large 7000 sq.m. call- and control-centre was built in 1993-5 to the design of Nicholas Grimshaw and Partners, an outstandingly brilliant firm of architects with a world reputation. The Supercentre has two functions: a practical one, to house 650 staff on three floors around an atrium; and a symbolic one, to serve as a landmark and a subtle advertisement for the RAC.

The design of the offices is a development of Grimshaw's slightly earlier Western Morning News Building in Plymouth. It is built on a curved triangular plan, with each floor projecting over the one below, and with the canted sheets of window glass protected by white sun shades. The roof is slightly domed and also white. When seen from a distance the building looks like a stack of three shallow saucers hovering low over the landscape. This particular landscape is a knot of motorways and a grunge of forgettable office buildings, but they are all dominated by this glorious intruder.

Curiously few organisations have taken advantage of the fact that bored drivers welcome landmarks on their motorway journeys, especially when they have to be undertaken regularly. Of those few landmarks that there are, some are geographical features, such as the Malvern Hills seen from the M5, and some are man-made but got there by chance, such as the radio mast at Membury on the M4. Examples which were deliberately positioned to be seen from a motorway, such as the Angel of the North, are rare, and all the more welcome. It was there-

space has to be taken up by corridors. Here there are none because the circulation space is the front part of each room. As a result the amount of internal privacy is limited, but since the house was designed by the architect for himself and his wife, that was what they wanted: a house that suits them perfectly but would not suit everybody.

This is one of the most beautiful Bristol buildings of the last 50 years. I couldn't live in it myself, but we all have our own personalities and ways of life. Michael Axford was lucky enough, and clever enough, to be able to build something which fits him and his wife to perfection, and can give those fortunate enough to see it an aesthetic pleasure of an unusual intensity.

fore canny of the RAC to develop a policy of building their regional supercentres beside motorways, and to make them as prominent and memorable as possible. It was typically brilliant of Nicholas Grimshaw, when he was asked to design this one at the junction of the M4 and M5, to turn up the screw by adding a spectacular observation mast.

The most obvious examples of buildings with a powerful symbolic message are churches. The thousands of spires throughout the land have no practical function whatever, but nobody mistakes their symbolic purpose. Most other types of buildings are symbolic to some extent, but it is unusual to find commercial ones which set out to convey any message other than crude success and power. Of course advertising is part of this RAC building's purpose, but it is done subtly, by suggesting that it is an organisation which watches, day and night, over the welfare of the motorists rushing by, ever ready to go to their help.

This building's spire is composed of two very tall steel masts. Suspended from them is a science fiction visitors' room giving views over the complex motorway junction and the Severn estuary beyond. It is perhaps just a little more practical than a church spire, but its symbolic, high-tech, function is paramount. Many of the millions of motorists who pass it each year will remember it more than they do the boring complexities of negotiating the motorway junction.

riverstation restaurant The Grove
1998

This inspired little building, with its lower case 'r', sits on the site of the old river police station, an unmemorable shed-like building with a slipway and tiny dock. The restaurant was built in 1998 to the design of Mike Richards of Inscape Architects.

There can be few more attractive inner-city sites for a restaurant. It looks out over a great expanse of water to the spectacular panorama of Redcliffe Parade on its red cliff; with St Mary Redcliffe towering up on the left, and dock cranes visible on the extreme right. The restaurant is built on two storeys, the lower of which bridges over the old dock and sits very gently on the listed quay. Both storeys have balconies wide enough to accept plenty of tables and chairs. In the 1980s and '90s many buildings in Bristol and elsewhere were given roofs of curving planes, few of which had any other justification than novelty. Many of them look absurd, on top of buildings to which they have no obvious relationship. I can recall none as successful as this one. When seen from the ferries plying constantly up and down the harbour, or from the quayside opposite, the building's maritime appearance is unmistakable, owing less to the sail-like roofs than to the overall marine functionalism and horizontality of the decks and their rails floating over the old police dock.

Internally the roof shells are an essential part of the first floor restaurant's attraction. The logic of the L-shaped space arranged around the kitchen is easily grasped, but the complexity of the roof is not, which is, perhaps, its greatest fascination. It is curious how the mind is attracted to visual complexity which is hard to grasp or understand, particularly when, as here, it contains an element of the irrational. A minor but very

real pleasure of the building is the quality of the detailing: the stair for example, and the toilets, are worth design awards of their own.

This little gem is one of my favourites amongst Bristol's late-twentieth-century buildings. The restaurant owes its great success to the quality of its cooking and the splendour of its location, but it also owes a very great deal to the pleasures of visiting a building of outstanding architectural quality.

Millennium Square

2000

The Square, which opened in 2000, was designed by the Concept Planning Group, a consortium of architects which at that time consisted of the practices, Alec French and Ferguson Mann Architects.

Europe's great urban squares are all spaces ringed by buildings, and the most visually satisfying are those where the height of the buildings is sufficient to provide

a sense of enclosure. That was never going to be possible in Millennium Square because only a part of the east side and the whole of the north side were occupied by buildings, with nothing on the other two sides. The way in which the architects dealt with this problem was highly ingenious. In fact it is unique, because Millennium Square is the only successful civic space in Britain which is part of a multi-storey car park: in fact its roof. The car park provided not only the surface of the Square but the additional elements needed to enclose it.

Multi-storey car parks are almost invariably inhuman and unpleasant, and underground ones are notoriously vile. This is the great exception, widely accepted as the most pleasant in Britain. The design of the stairs, lifts, wall surfaces and signage, and above all, the control of the workmanship, has produced a notably friendly and welcoming atmosphere.

The north side of the Square is closed by Explore At-Bristol, reflected in its great pool. Most of the south side is occupied by the building housing the stairs and lifts to the car park, and the east and west sides are enclosed by a series of towers reminiscent of the cooling wind towers of north Africa. Their function is very similar to them; they contain the car park's ventilation ducts. There is something particularly satisfying in the way that the car park provides so many of the elements which make the Square visually successful. It is made popular by a number of works of art, ranging from one of my favourites, a little, absolutely realistic, Jack Russell terrier, which was stolen, returned and can now be seen inside the entrance to the Explore building; a figure of Cary Grant which doesn't do much for me, along with others;

successful is the informal Anchor Square opening off its north-east corner, which is filled with restaurants and tables in the open air. That in turn connects to the always bustling quaysides along the Floating Harbour. By a very large margin this complex is the city's most successful piece of planning, achieved by employing gifted architects instead of inevitably ungifted bureaucrats in its own employment.

the glorious, always sparkling, sphere of the Planetarium; and William Pye's superlative complex of fountains: a series of mirror walls down which sheets of water flow, miraculously smoothly, into pools. Both these large works of art are enormously popular, with adults as well as children. For once officialdom allows, or turns a blind eye to, children paddling and touching the mirror surfaces. On warm sunny days there are few places in Bristol as delightful as Millennium Square.

It is only the largest of a sequence of interconnecting spaces designed by the Concept Planning Group. Just as

Explore At-Bristol   Anchor Square, Harbourside
1904, 2000

Canon's Marsh was the termination of the Great West-ern Railway's line into the docks. The site of Explore At-Bristol was a 1906 goods shed, a remarkably unat-tractive building listed because of its reinforced concrete structure, which consisted of a series of cross walls, arched to allow the passage of the trains. It was designed by Louis-Gustave Mouchel, using the system designed —by one of the great nineteenth-century engineers, François Hennebique, for whom Mouchel was the

west end of the new building. The science centre's façade facing the street is a huge two-storey wall of glass, allow-ing passers-by to see the attractions within. It is damaged by the vast lettering announcing the name of the building. The south side, facing onto Millennium Square, is separated from it by a long pool. A bridge on the first floor leads to the Planetarium, housed in an enormous globe faced with facetted sheets of polished stainless steel, giving endlessly fascinating broken reflec-tions. It is quite probable that this huge distorting mirror gives as much pleasure to adults and children as the planetarium inside it.

English agent. Hennebique began life as a farm labourer, became a stonemason, built up a huge construction company and first used reinforced concrete in 1879. He built the first concrete bridge in 1894 and the first grain elevator in 1895. The Canon's Marsh goods shed, for which the drawings are dated 1904, is a very early use of reinforced concrete in Britain. Its preservation is obvi-ously important.

Explore At-Bristol, a hands-on science centre, was completed in 2000 to the design of Chris Wilkinson Architects. The Hennebique concrete structure is far from handsome (it was, after all, never intended to be seen) so they embedded most of it within the new build-ing, allowing just one of its arched walls to be seen as the

Office for Lloyds Banking Group

Canon's Marsh, Harbourside

2007

When containerization finally killed the Bristol City Docks, an enormous amount of land in the central area lost its purpose, the largest chunk of which was Canon's Marsh. From the late 1960s onwards there were several plans for its redevelopment, all of which were aborted because they proved to be hopelessly unrealistic. The situation was only resolved when the Council appointed an outside consultant, the architect Ted Cullinan, to

atrium: a huge fascinating space enlivened by a free-standing tower of stair and lifts placed off-centre. Its long south-facing façade on the waterfront is the most interesting, and by far the most attractive on this length of the quay. Its lowest and top storeys are recessed, and the intermediate three are faced by a huge louvred sun-screen, so that they seem to float above the quay wall. The fully glazed, pavilion-like top floor, which is set back behind the screen, makes a most satisfying cap on the building.

The Lloyds office is included in this book primarily because of the architectural distinction of its quayside

draw up proposals. Basically, his masterplan for the area proposed a multi-storey development of varying heights arranged about two wide avenues. One provides a vista from Millennium Square to the ss *Great Britain*, the other a vista from an arbitrarily chosen spot on the opposite bank of the harbour to the Cathedral. The result, as it has finally emerged, has pleased nobody. Bristol Civic Society wanted everything to be low-rise; my own view is that, contrary to Cullinan's wishes, there is not enough variety in the heights of the buildings. Everybody appears to agree that the general architectural level is undistinguished. Fortunately one or two buildings stand out.

The best is the 2007 office for the Lloyds Banking Group designed by the large international architectural practice Aukett Fitzroy Robinson. Its five storeys occupy almost every foot of its triangular site, extending right into the corners. The three sides enclose a glass-roofed

façade, but it is also fascinating for another reason. Harbour water is taken into the building through grilles in the quay wall, passed into heat exchangers in the basement, and used to provide free cooling through chilled beams above the suspended ceilings. Fresh air is supplied to the offices through floor voids and extracted at high level. Solar collectors on the roof heat the domestic hot water, and excessive solar heat gain is controlled by the external louvres. The result is a very efficient, attractive, building.

Cabot Circus and Quakers' Friars

2008

In the years leading up to the Millennium, a remarkable enterprise was being planned in Bristol; the building of Cabot Circus. There is nothing unusual about planning a new shopping centre, but this one was based on an extraordinarily bold concept. More and more people were being attracted away from Broadmead to the easy car parking of Cribb's Causeway, so the obvious thing to do was to extend Broadmead and provide more parking: obvious but seemingly impossible. The trouble was that it was ringed by apparently insuperable barriers: the high property values and numerous listed buildings on its west; Castle Park on its south; and the Inner Circuit Road on its north and east. The bold decision was to alter the line of the Ring Road by extending its circuit eastward. That involved a great deal of expensive property acquisition, the colossal expense of building a great length of multi-lane highway and its complex junctions, and the huge expense of diverting all the services which ran beneath the old road. After that everything must have seemed straight-forward.

Cabot Circus opened in September 2008. It was designed by Chapman Taylor Architects, specialists in large retail and other urban developments. It consists of a large multi-level central hub and three multi-level malls which connect the new development with the old Broadmead. The hub is connected to a huge multi-storey car park. The malls and the hub are roofed by ten over-lapping curved glass shells which never connect with each other and are independent from the buildings supporting them, thereby providing gaps for ventilation and the escape of smoke in the event of fire. The roof of the central hub is a fan-shaped torus, and like all pure mathematical forms, extremely beautiful. The shape of the other nine shells is much more arbitrary, and their relationship to each other, and to the spaces and buildings, seems wilful and illogical. The explanation is that the whole roof is a gigantic work of art, conceived by the installation artist Nayan Kulkarni. Presumably he produced models of what he wanted, but of course everything had to be designed in detail, calculated, and no doubt adapted, by the consultant engineer, SKM Hunt. Perhaps it was an admirable idea to use an artist in this way, but in my opinion the experiment has failed. The roofs would have looked better if they had been conceived and designed by the architects and engineers working together in the normal way, and in consequence were less wilfully 'different'.

The complex consists of several levels of shops, connected at numerous places by bridges, stairs and escalators. It adds up to one of the most exciting interiors in Britain and must be judged an enormous success. When seen on a busy Saturday, thronged with people going up and down escalators and moving across glass bridges at different heights and angles, it is the Futurists' dream realized at last, exactly a century after Marinetti launched his famous Manifesto and he and his followers produced images which now seem extraordinarily prophetic.

There was an aesthetic price to be paid for this success. The backs of the shops and stores face onto the inner ring road, in other words onto drivers not window-shoppers. Of necessity most of the buildings along this stretch of road are tall and windowless: an enormously difficult architectural problem. Chapman Taylor tried to humanise these hundreds of metres of wall by using a multitude of materials, textures and overlapping surfaces, but the result is not successful and is much criticised in Bristol.

However, people drive heedlessly past the wall and stroll fascinated and happy through the malls inside. As far as one can see, Cabot Circus is an enormous commercial success, with only a tiny number of shop units unlet. To go from there to the old Broadmead is a painful experience. There the streets are cluttered with squalid shacks and trailers selling cheap goods and snacks: the malls in Cabot Circus are immaculate, mercifully free from visually illiterate municipal attempts to screw a few more pennies in rents, whatever the real cost.

One part of the old Broadmead – Quakers' Friars – was given a long overdue rebuilding as part of the same development. This part of the exercise was designed by the Bristol architectural practice, Alec French Architects. Previously all the shops faced onto the surrounding roads and turned their ugly backs onto Quakers' Friars. When wedding guests left the Register Office they were faced by rows of dustbins and refuse sacks. The architects demolished the surrounding buildings and replaced them with beautifully designed shops and flats which now face onto the great open space. They also restored the Friends' Meeting House and the adjoining medieval Bakers' Hall in the centre, giving them back the beauty they lost in the 1950s. The

result is a resounding success: Quakers' Friars is now one of the most beautiful open spaces in the city.*

Although I hope towns and villages will always have corner shops and short rows of local shops, I am convinced that developments like Cabot Circus and Quakers' Friars are the future of mainstream shopping in Britain. Together they contain a huge number of small shops and large stores, they provide protection from the rain and the opportunity to sit and eat in the sun, they supply many of the entertainments for adults and children that a city can provide – in this case a cinema, cafés, restaurants, even indoor golf – but being embedded in the city, the vast range of other urban facilities are available only a short walk away. They provide access to car parking without having to walk through the rain to get there. They bring vitality and revenue into the city instead of sucking them out, as the out-of-town shopping centres do. In only one way do they appear to offer less: shoppers have to pay for their parking whilst those shopping out of town think they don't (though of course they do, but indirectly). If that could be solved, the out-of-town shopping centres would face a real challenge.

* In 1974, as part of my commission from the City Council to advise on the pedestrianisation of Broadmead, I proposed to glass-roof the streets and turn back-to-front the shops around Quakers' Friars. Both were rejected almost unanimously by the traders. It takes a generation or more to get new ideas lodged in conservative minds.

Broad Quay

2009

Most of the 'comprehensive redevelopments' so strongly promoted by planners in the 1960s are now recognized to have been failures because they obliterated large areas of little buildings, often of much character, and replaced them with two or three large blocks of uniform character. However, developers today still sometimes buy or assemble sites containing a number of buildings which are judged to be obsolete and requiring renewal. This Broad Quay development is one such, though of much more limited size than most of the early ones. Its interest is partly its architectural quality but also the care taken to avoid the mistakes of the 1960s.

Like most ancient streets Broad Quay has a long history of redevelopment. The quay and the buildings along it were built in the 1240s when the Frome was diverted into its present course. Since then the buildings have been subject to continual replacement as needs and maritime trading patterns changed. In 1698, for example, it saw the first brick building in Bristol (demolished in the nineteenth century). Over the last 30 or 40 years Broad Quay's buildings were looking increasingly sad and it was becoming obvious that new ones and new uses were needed.

The spur to the present redevelopment was the 1966 Bristol and West tower. When the building society moved out, its narrow floors were judged to be uneconomic by modern office tenants and it found no new occupants. Demolition or change of use became inevitable. It was found that its overall shape would be suitable for a hotel, though nothing but the structural frame of columns and floors would be usable. The Bristol architects AWW therefore stripped it down to these bones and rebuilt it. Working with Softroom, a practice specializing in public art, they designed the fascinating new cladding. It grades in tones of grey and blue from dark at the bottom to pale at the top. The effect is quite extraordinary because the tower seems to merge into the sky as it rises upward. Towers are rarely popular these days but this newly transformed one seems already to have achieved popular success in Bristol.

The site was much larger than merely the tower. In addition to the hotel it now accommodates 196 flats and

a few shops, which give it long frontages on Broad Quay and Marsh Street. The danger was that a '60s type of design would be adopted whereby everything would be squeezed into two or three large blocks. That has been avoided. The height of the previous buildings along the Quay and in Marsh Street is maintained by three storeys of shops and flats along the ancient building line, all faced with Bath stone. The scale of the individual old buildings is maintained by this long façade being treated as a series of slim vertical elements. All the accommodation above these three storeys is set back behind them and divided into separate blocks, building up in height to the tower. The effect is a group of buildings behind the street façade.

At the point where the Quay and Marsh Street meet, the building is treated as a six-storey drum, and all the accommodation steps back from it, storey by storey, up to the tower. The roof slab of each storey projects well beyond the building below it. The view of this from Prince Street (below) is stunning.

Avon Meads Bridge Temple Quay
2008

The arrival of computers in designers' offices has been responsible for a revolution in architecture and structural engineering. The several millennia reign of the set square, the tee square and the right angle has come to a close. This is nowhere more apparent than in the crop of bridges built over the last 30 years or so. Bristol has several whose construction would previously have been impossible because their calculations would have been too complex even to contemplate. One of the more attractive and interesting of them is this footbridge over the Floating Harbour where it runs under the tracks leaving Temple Meads Station.

Its attractiveness is apparent to everybody: its interest lies in the way that the design was an unusually creative collaboration between the architect, the engineer and the lighting consultant – Niall McLaughlin, Price and Myers and Martin Richman respectively. It was decided early on that the bridge was to be entirely of steel, with no other materials whatever. The skeleton of the bridge is a grid of steel beams with triangular upstands to support the sides of the bridge. The stressed skin which wraps around these bones is 6mm high-quality rigid stainless-steel plate which provides a high proportion of the strength – as in the aluminium skin of an aircraft's wing. This meant that the bridge was stiff enough to be fabricated off-site and lifted whole into position by a crane.

The lighting consultant contributed a wonderful idea, that the lights should be installed within the carcass and the skin pierced by circular holes to provide illumination along its length. This was fine, but piercing the skin could obviously result in the bridge's collapse as soon as the stresses of spanning 55 metres, and carrying a potentially large number of people, were imposed on it. In order to make it possible the engineers were pitchforked into entirely new territory and had to use aerospace software, amongst others, in order to develop their own software. Not surprisingly, it emerged that there were places in the skin which could not be pierced at all, others where only small holes were possible, and a few where they could be up to 40mm in diameter. The calculations for this would have been impossible before the introduction of computers. The result, an extraordinarily complex pattern of 55,000 holes of different

diameters and spacing, is enchanting; fascinating in daylight and magical at night. As Niall McLaughlin has said, the pattern is a map of the stresses which are acting on the skin.

However, as everybody who has a stainless steel sink knows, stainless steel may be stainless, but it does require constant cleaning and polishing to keep its shine. That is not likely to be humanly available at Meads Reach, and rain doesn't appear to be doing the job. After two years exposure there are a few places where the steel is becoming unpleasantly dirty. It will be interesting to see how this works out.

HQ, Aardman Animations Gas Ferry Road
2009

Aardman built its world reputation whilst housed in a former banana warehouse and a few portacabins on a site on Spike Island, the long strip of land between the Floating Harbour and the New Cut. Continual growth led them to stage a limited competition to find an architect to prepare a master plan for their site, which included adjoining land. The competition was won by

boarding, the apparently random placing of the bay windows and the vertical and horizontal strip windows, make an endlessly fascinating and complex façade. A similar treatment is used throughout the exterior of the building, which stretches back from the road.

Aardman's large-scale production takes place in industrial sheds elsewhere in the city. The administrative

the Bristol-based Alec French Architects, who were then commissioned to design a new building facing onto Gas Ferry Road. Its construction was completed in February 2009.

Gas Ferry Road is built-up along its west side but formless on the east, most of its length being occupied by a large surface car park and a little banana warehouse previously isolated near its southern end. This part of the street has now been pulled together by the entrance façade of the new three-storey Aardman building which adjoins the banana warehouse. The new building's main facing material – larch and chestnut boarding – is unusual on an urban site. It will weather to a beautiful silver colour to harmonise with the matt-glazed tiles and copper-clad bay windows. The varied patterns of the

and creative work is done in the new building. The key to this is the free and informal exchange of ideas between directors and members of staff, which, it was decided, could best take place in a series of linked rooms, each containing working groups of six to nine people. These are arranged on either side of a three-storey tapered atrium and accessed from galleries looking onto it.

Visitors to the building enter the atrium, which is spectacular. Rising through the three storeys and flooded by daylight from the largely glass roof, it is a highly complex volume, impossible to comprehend in a quick glance. The basic arrangement is simple, a space tapering away from the entrance, with galleries rising on each side and a central stairway curving up to the first floor. But this simplicity is enormously complicated – by the way

the space curves out of sight at the back; by the orange and yellow break-out balconies projecting from the first and second floor galleries; and perhaps most of all, by the complexity of the exposed structure.

Both inside and out the arrangement of each feature seems at first glance wilful, but when you examine them closely it becomes clear that they are in fact positioned and designed logically. The cumulative effect is intensely stimulating – a beautiful, fascinating headquarters for a company producing beautiful, imaginative films.

Alphabetical list of buildings

Selected list of people, firms and institutions

Redcliffe Press: further reading

Bristol Central Library and Charles Holden
Anthony Beeson

A Bristol Eye: the city seen from new perspectives
Tim Mowl and Stephen Morris

Bristol Before the Camera: the city in 1820-30
Sheena Stoddard

Bristol's Floating Harbour
Peter Malpass and Andy King

C20/21: Bristol's modern buildings
Tony Aldous

Discovering Harbourside: A Journey to the Heart of Bristol
James Russell and Stephen Morris

From Bristol to the Sea
Francis Greenacre

In Search of Bristol
Stephen Morris

Open Doors: Bristol's Hidden Interiors
Tim Mowl and Stephen Morris

A Palladian Villa in Bristol: Clifton Hill House
Annie Burnside

The Paty Family: Makers of Eighteenth-Century Bristol
Gordon Priest

Public View: A Profile of the Royal West of England Academy
John Sansom (ed)

Queen Square
Andrew Kelly

St Mary Redcliffe: A Church and its People
Peter Aughton

Sculpture in Bristol
Douglas Merritt

Sir George Oatley: Bristol's Architect
Sarah Whittingham

To Build the Second City: Architects and Craftsmen of Georgian Bristol
Tim Mowl

The authors

Michael Jenner

Whilst a Lecturer at Bath University, in 1958 Mike Jenner co-founded Moxley, Jenner and Partners, eventually a large national practice of architects, planners and landscapists, winners of 14 awards, commendations or competitions. In 1986 he started a consultancy to advise local authorities, property developers and amenity societies on developments in sensitive locations, appearing as an expert witness on many occasions. In 1979 he was joint author of the standard history of Bristol's architecture and in the '70s and '80s he made 53 television films on architecture. In 1989 he was appointed Architectural and Planning Advisor to Bristol Development Corporation. For 20 years until 2004 he was a member of Bristol University's Court, its ultimate governing body.

Stephen Morris

Stephen is a commercial photographer, writer and designer, and editor of the *Bristol Review of Books*. He was born in Liverpool. He now lives in Bristol and has produced several books for Redcliffe Press and the (irreverent) history of *Cheltenham*, with photographs, for Frances Lincoln.

e-book
The publishers are looking into the option of publishing this book in electronic format for readers who would welcome a portable version. Visit: www.redcliffepress.co.uk